Stationary Steam Engines of Great Britain
The National Photographic Collection
Volume 3.1: Lancashire

George Watkins

The Watkins' Collection in the National Monuments Record

This comprises the photographs and notes George Watkins made during a lifetime of study of the stationary steam engine.

The Steam Engine Record is an annotated set of around 1500 mounted prints of steam engines which Watkins examined in the field between 1930 and 1980. His notebooks contain a record of additional sites for which no photographs were taken, or which comprise written historical notes. In all almost 2000 entries were made in his notebooks. There are also albums of prints arranged by engine type. A catalogue is available.

In addition there are files of notes and other records on all aspects of historical steam technology, the cataloguing of which is in progress.

The main areas of this part of the collection are:

Records of steam engine makers.

Collection of bound trade literature.

Classified collection of data files dealing with, for example, textile mill engines, marine engines.

The collection can be inspected by appointment. Copies of photographs and other documents are readily available.

Please contact:

NMR Enquiry & Research Services
National Monuments Record Centre
Kemble Drive
Swindon
Wilts
SN2 2GZ

STATIONARY STEAM ENGINES OF GREAT BRITAIN

THE NATIONAL PHOTOGRAPHIC COLLECTION

VOLUME 3.1: LANCASHIRE

George Watkins

Landmark Publishing

Published by
Landmark Publishing Ltd,
Ashbourne Hall, Cokayne Ave, Ashbourne, Derbyshire DE6 1EJ England
Tel: (01335) 347349 Fax: (01335) 347303
e-mail: landmark@clara.net
web site: www.landmarkpublishing.co.uk

ISBN 1 901522 56 3

© George Watkins

Print: MPG Ltd, Bodmin, Cornwall
Designed by: James Allsopp
Editor: A P Woolrich
Production: C L M Porter

Front cover: The Gorse Mill, Chadderton, nr. Oldham, SER 603
Back cover: Harwoods, Cotton Spinners, Bolton, SER 751 (2)
Page 3: Glenby Mill, Chadderton, nr. Oldham, SER 498

CONTENTS

FOREWORD
by A. P. Woolrich

George Watkins (1904-1989) spent most of his working life as a heating engineer and boilerman in Bristol. Starting in the 1930's, in his spare time he made short trips throughout Britain photographing and recording stationary steam engines. In 1965, aged 61, he was appointed a research assistant at the Centre for the Study of the History of Technology at Bath University, under Dr R. A. Buchanan, and was enabled to devote all his time adding to and classifying his collection. He was still making field trips until the late 1970's, when ill-health made travelling difficult.

He was an occasional contributor to *Model Engineer*, and other periodicals and wrote important papers for the *Transactions of the Newcomen Society*. Following his appointment to Bath University he was in much demand as a lecturer and produced a series of books based on his research. These were:

The Stationary Steam Engine (1968)

The Textile Mill Engine, 2 Vol, (1970, 1971), 2ed, (1999)

Man and the Steam Engine, (1975), 2 imp (1978) (with R. A. Buchanan)

The Industrial Archaeology of the Stationary Steam Engine, (1976) (with R. A. Buchanan)

The Steam Engine in Industry 2 vol, (1978, 1979)

On his death in February 1989 his collection was gifted to the Royal Commission on the Historical Monuments of England.

It may be freely consulted at English Heritage's National Record Centre at Swindon. As well as photographs the collection comprises numerous technical notes about all manner of steam engine related topics; an incomparable archive of trade catalogues, some dating from the late nineteenth century; a collection of letters from like-minded friends, of value today for the light they shed on the history of the growth of Industrial Archaeology; lecture notes and slides. His library was left to Bath University.

He would visit a site and take illustrated notes and photographs, usually around half a dozen. His notes usually contained measured sketches of the machines and also the layouts of the premises he visited. In all, he travelled over 120,000 miles and visited nearly 2000 sites, but in approximately 10% only took written notes. He filed sets of contact prints of each visit in binders sorted by engine type and between 1965-1971 he made a selection of the best prints for Bath University staff to print to a larger format. These were drymounted on card and annotated with details from his field notebooks and today form what is known at the Steam Engine Record. It is this collection, with notes, which forms the basis of the present series of regional books.

The Steam Engine Record is filed in numerical order, but catalogues are available listing makers, engine types and locations. When the field trips were being made the historic county names still applied, but the modern catalogues in the Search Room at Swindon allow searching by new counties and metropolitan areas, such as Cleveland and

Greater Manchester. In this series, how-ever, the historical county names have been retained.

When he began his surveys, he travelled by bicycle and train, and many were to sites he could reach readily from Bristol, but he soon graduated to a series of autocycles, on which he would pack his photographic gear and his clothing. He planned his trips meticulously during the winter months, writing to mill own-ers to gain permission, and then during following summer (when his boiler was shut down for maintenance), having saved up all his available leave time, would then spend two or three weeks on his travels, staying in bed-and-breakfast accommodation, or, as he became more widely known, with friends. During the autumn he would write up his notes, and begin planning the following year's trip.

He was initially interested in beam engines, but soon concentrated on the textile mill engines of mostly Lancashire and Yorkshire. In this he was greatly aided by local experts such as Frank Wightman and Arthur Roberts, who were working in these areas. Later his interest included colliery winding engines, waterworks and marine engines. During the War, when he found difficulty in both travel-ling far and in getting permission to enter industrial sites, he investigated water-powered sites, such as the Avon Valley brass mills, near Bristol, and the Worcestershire edge tool manufacturing sites. An area of steam technology which did not concern him was the railway lo-comotive, though he did record a small number of industrial locomotives and traction engines he found on his visits.

The regional distribution of the sites he visited includes most English counties and a number in Wales and Scotland. The numbers of sites he saw in the counties differ greatly, with Yorkshire, Lancashire, and the counties around Bristol predomi-nating. This is because he had close links with other workers in those areas, and

he relied on this network to learn where engines might be found. Areas where he had few contacts tended to be thinly covered.

In many counties he saw sites with a marine connection. These will be covered in Volume 10 of this series. In this con-text this means a steam engine which drove a vessel, whether at sea, river or canal. Also preserved marine engines. Engines at waterside features such as dockside workshops are included in the regional sequence of books.

George Watkins often photographed under near impossible conditions. Engine-room lighting was frequently indifferent, and confined space often made hard the siting of the camera for obtaining adequate perspective views. For most of the work reproduced in this series he used a tripod-mounted wooden plate camera with extension bellows which he modified to accept different lenses. In his early years he was con-tinually experimenting with different com-binations of film speeds, lenses and exposure times. Although he did even-tually own a 35mm roll film camera, he was never happy with using it, and was frequently heard to grumble about the quality of modern film stock.

He used cut film, held in a dark slide, and had the films developed by a local chemist in the centres he visited so he could go back and take another if a print failed. He overcame bad lighting by having very long exposures, so was able to appear in his own prints occasionally.

The long exposures also meant he was able to 'freeze' a slow-moving engine. He did this by shielding the lens by a hand-held card or the lens cap until the engine had reached, say, top dead centre and then removing the shield momentarily. This cumulative exposure resulted in an image of a still engine, and such was his deftness of touch and impeccable timing, that it is very hard to see any kind of shake or blemish on the photographs. He was adept at 'painting with light' -

utilising hand-held electric lead-lights with which he could illuminate different parts of the engine successively.

He made copies from his negatives at home for distribution to his friends by using a simple contact-print frame and developer chemicals. There are many small sets of his prints in private hands.

The lenses he used were not bloomed to prevent 'flaring' of the image caused by extraneous light from windows or hanging light bulbs, and some of the photographs reproduced are marred by this. He made his selection of prints for the Steam Engine Record on the basis of their historical and technical importance, and not on their artistic quality.

His photographs are a unique record of the end of stationary steam power in this country, being made at a time when electrification, nationalisation and trade depression created wholesale changes in the physical structure of the industrial landscape. They are an invaluable resource to our understanding of the reality of industrial activity, and will interest, as well as the technical historian, the local historian and model-maker. It is good to know they are being published, for this in turn will focus attention on the rest of his reference collection, which deserves to be more widely known and used.

ISSES (The International Stationary Steam Engine Society) is publishing a number of volumes devoted to George Watkins and his work. They will include a short biography, memoirs from several of his friends, a bibliography of his writings and reprints of his articles.

Details may be obtained from:

Mr John Cooper,
73 Coniston Way,
Blossom Hill,
Bewdley, Worcestershire,
DY12 2QA
Tel: 01299 402946

Email:
John.Cooper@isses2.freeserve.co.uk

Web site: www.steamenginesociety.org

The layout of this book follows the same pattern as the publisher's re-issue of *The Textile Mill Engine*, namely a page of three sets of notes followed by three full page photographs illustrating those notes. A little editing has been done to ensure consistency, but the texts are as George Watkins wrote them. It is pointed out, however that they were written over thirty years ago, and were often based on observations made thirty to forty years before that.

Many of the sites, if they now exist at all, have been radically altered, and very few of the engines and machines he saw now survive. A handful of engines are preserved in museums, such as the Bradford Industrial Museum, and societies such as ISSES and the Northern Mill Engine Society maintain records of engines in private hands.

The sites are in alphabetical order of place, and then site owner or site name and no attempt has been made to identify them by precise grid references. Each entry heading has an illustration number for this volume, the location details as recorded on the original record card, and the Steam Engine Record (SER) number. This latter number is the key for accessing the copies of the field notebooks and the files of additional photographs in the National Monuments Record at Swindon. The SER number comprises a four digit number (which mirrors the numbering of the field notebooks) and sometimes an additional alphabetical letter. These relate to additional prints of the same site prepared for the mounted set of prints. The photographs in the contact print books and the original negatives are not so numbered.

LANCSHIRE

Lancashire contains the largest number of sites George Watkins visited. The two volumes published here contain approx 320 photographs and the *Textile Mill Engine* a further 83 not reproduced here. The bulk of the visits were to textile mills, and the engines he saw drove a wide range of equipment in premises which covered all the ramifications of the industry. These ranged from entire mill complexes, driven by a single engine, to smaller engines which formed part of an individual machine within a mill, such as a tenterer or a calender.

There was even one site whose sole occupation was to wash and recycle the oily cloths used by the engineers who tended the engines and mill machinery.

Another block of sites concerned mining, and other blocks included water-powered mills and a small number of industrial locomotives.

From the 1950's the cotton trade had gone into severe decline in the face of foreign imports, and the growth of the use of man-made fibres. In 1959 the Government introduced legislation to compensate cotton manufacturers who wished to reduce their capacity - the cotton spindles redundancy scheme. This resulted in a drastic scrapping of equipment, and George Watkins's notes are a continual record of the decline of the industry since then.

With his friend Frank Wightman, he had made in 1964 a report on the Lancashire textile mill engines for Rex Wailes, who at that time was running a scheme for the Ministry of Works to identify significant industrial monuments for preservation. This was, of course in advance of the later Industrial Archaeology movement. Frank Wightman was a lifelong friend, who greatly helped in George Watkins's work, sending him information about mills and machines, and, in later times, newspaper cuttings about impending closures, which he preserved in his records.

George Watkins later published two books of photographs of textile mill engines, covering mostly Lancashire and Yorkshire, but including other counties as well.

In his notes he mentions the activities of a couple of independent engine designers, employed by engine makers. J. H. Tattersall established himself as a consulting engineer in Preston at the close of the nineteenth century. He designed the triple-expansion beam engines for the renowned Nile Mill at Hollinwood. Another designer, was a Mr Nuekomm, a Swiss national with expertise in Continental drop-valve engines, who worked for John Petrie & Co, Ltd in the early twentieth century.

FURTHER READING

D. A. Collier, 'A comparative history of the development of the leading stationary steam engine manufacturers of Lancashire c 1800-1939', (PhD Thesis, 1985).

C. Aspin, *The Cotton Industry*, 1981.

T. C. Dickinson, *Lancashire under steam: the era of the steam-driven cotton mill*, 1984.

D. Gurr and J. Hunt, *The Cotton Mills of Oldham*, 1988.

L. H. C. Tippett, *A portrait of the Lancashire Textile Industry*, 1969.

Mike Williams with D. A. Farnie, *Cotton mills in Greater Manchester*, 1992.

Beam engine, the original form as made by Boulton and Watt. This form owed its existence to the fact that all the earlier steam engines were used for pumping water, the beam forming a convenient means of attachment for the pump rods.

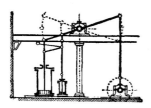

Horizontal Engine, with open frame cast iron bedplate, a type much used for all sizes of engine for general purposes. The bed-plate frame was of a U section, and was bolted down to a foundation of masonry or brickwork, the cylinder, main bearing and guides being bolted to the bed-plate.

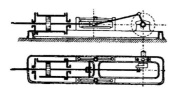

Vertical engine, a type used extensively for both large and small engines; it had the advantage of occupying little floor space. An endless number of varieties of this type was developed, and was the generally accepted type for marine screw-propeller engines.

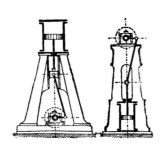

Corliss frame or Girder Engine, a type of horizontal engine. This example had a bored guide, but they were also made with flat-planed guides. In both cases the guides were formed in the main casting or girder which connects the cylinder to the main bearing. There were many varieties of this type.

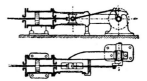

Self contained horizontal engines, with bent or slotted out cranks. This type, largely used for small power short-stroke engines had the cylinder bolted on to the end of an open bed-plate, which was widened out at the other end to take both bearings of the crank shaft, so that the flywheel might be keyed on either side. The guides were usually formed in the bedplate, the boring out of the guides and facing of the end flange being done at the same setting.

Oscillating Engines, formerly much used as marine engines. Originally developed for driving paddle wheels, this type has also been used for driving screw propellers. Uncommon in land use.

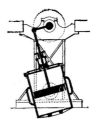

Steeple engine, formerly used for driving paddle wheels. A variety of this type had been used for small powers, and was known as the Table Engine.

Beam Engine, Woolf's Compound. Two unequal cylinders side by side, at one end of the beam. Many pumping engines were of this type.

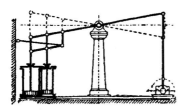

McNaught Compound Beam Engine. This system consisted of a small cylinder (high-pressure cylinder), placed at the opposite end of the beam to the larger cylinder, was introduced by McNaught for increasing the power of existing engines. The high-pressure cylinder was the one added, the original cylinder being the low-pressure cylinder. The power of the engine was thus increased by increase of boiler pressure and the addition of the new small cylinder, to which the boiler was admitted. (See glossary for more details).

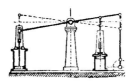

Inclined Frame Engines, used extensively for paddle steamers in several different varieties, usually compound engines.

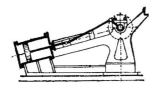

A Double-Cylinder Engine, derived from the above, with the cylinder inclined at an angle of about 45⁰, was occasionally used for driving rolling mills in bar iron works.

Radial Engines. (Brotherhood type) A recent type, of which there were many varieties, in both 3 and 4 cylinder configurations. These were used for driving fans, steam launches and other applications requiring speed and compactness.

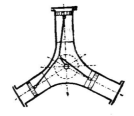

Central Valve Engines (Willans type) A modern design, single acting, compound or triple expansion configuration; a special feature was the hollow piston rod and central valve. Extensively used for driving dynamos coupled direct on to the armature shaft.

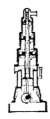

Various ways of arranging cylinders and cranks in double and three-cylinder compound and triple expansion engines

Double cylinder, with cranks at 180^0

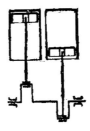

Three-cylinder engine, with cranks at 120^0

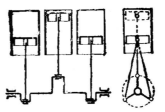

Compound Woolf engine with cranks together

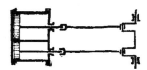

Compound Woolf engine with cranks at 180°

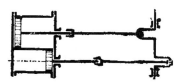

Compound Tandem engine with receiver

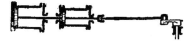

Compound engine with cylinders side by side with receiver cranks at 90°

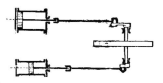

Triple expansion engine with cylinders side by side; cranks at 120°

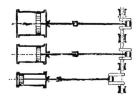

Triple expansion engine, semi-tandem; two cranks at 90°

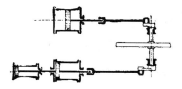

VALVES AND VALVE GEARS

Simple slide valve
This consisted of an inverted metal box sliding on the ported face of the cylinder. It controlled the admission and exhaust of the steam to both ends of the cylinder and exhausted beneath the box valve

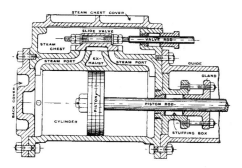

Simple piston valve
This consisted of a turned bobbin, working in a bored liner. It worked on the same principle as the slide valve.

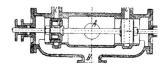

Simple valve gears
These valves were operated by simple eccentric motions of various patterns, and many allowed variable cut-off of the steam as well as reversing.

The Corliss
This was a semi-circular semi-rotating valve working in a bored liner. Separate valves were provided for steam and exhaust at each end of the cylinder, so there were four in number. A trip gear operated the valves.

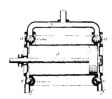

Drop valves

These were circular with taper faces, which fitted upon similar faces fitted to the cylinder. The faces were ground together to make them steam tight. The valves were lifted to admit steam and dropped by the trip gear to cut off the admission. A variety of this pattern was simple bobbins fitted with piston rings.

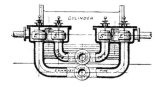

The Uniflow

This had admission valves only since the steam exhausted through a ring of ports in the centre of the cylinder barrel.

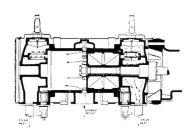

BOILERS

Cornish boilers contained a single flue

 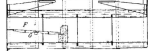

Lancashire boilers contained twin flues

 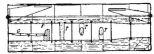

Multitibular boilers were of various types including the locomotive

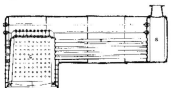

Vertical boilers were of various types. Used in very small plants

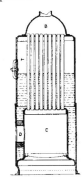

Watertube boilers were of various types.

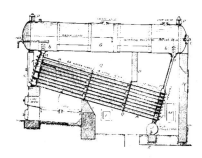

POWER TRANSMISSION

Rope drives, taking power from the engine to the floors of a mill, were usual in textile mills. In older mills power was often transmitted by a vertical shaft.

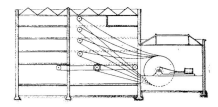

Flat belts of leather or rubberized canvas drove individual machines from a line shaft powered by the rope drive.

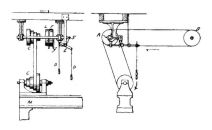

Winding engines were almost invariably made with two cylinders having cranks at **90⁰**, allowing good control by the engine driver. A winding engine was required to work intermittently, starting a heavy load from rest, bringing this load up with great velocity, and bringing it to rest again. This had to be done at great speed in a short time, since a great number of winds were needed daily to raise an economic quantity of coal. For this, the engine needed to be powerful and to be under precise control of the engineman at all times.

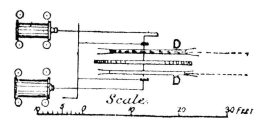

Balancing was done by fixing a rope similar to the winding rope to the bottom of each cage, the rope hanging in a loop down the pit shaft, ensuring a perpetual balance-weight equal to the winding-rope.

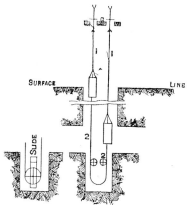

Another method of balancing was by means of the scroll or spiral drum. As the engine proceeded to wind up, the rope was wound in spiral grooves on a continually increasing diameter of drum. The other rope to the descending cage was wound off at an opposing rate so creating a counterbalance. The variation in diameter of the two sides of the drum had the effect of loading the engine proportional to the effort it needed at different stages of the wind.

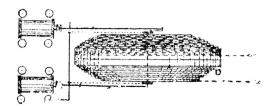

Winding was done by steam, utilising different types of pithead gear.

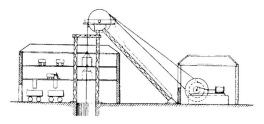

Ventilation was done by various patterns of steam driven rotary fan.

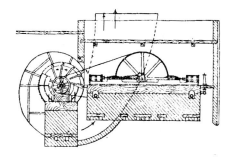

GLOSSARY

Air pump. This removed the condensed water and air contained in the steam. It was normally driven by the engine itself.

Arbor. An axle or spindle.

Barring. This was the action of gently rotating the engine to make possible adjustments during maintenance. It was done by a lever mechanism which engaged in a series of holes cast in the face or side of the flywheel rim. A variation involved a hand or small steam engine-driven gear engaging in gear teeth cast on the inside of the flywheel rim.

Calender. A finishing machine designed to impart lustre and smoothness to woven fabrics. It comprised a series of rolls geared vertically, through which the cloth ran.

Condensers. These were airtight chambers into which the exhaust steam passed for cooling back to warm water. Cooling was by a jet of cold water which mixed with the condensate, or, in the surface type, the cold water passed through a number of small tubes to condense the steam outside them.

Count. The measure of yarns by length and weight stating how many hanks of a given length will weigh a pound: the higher the number, the finer the yarn. There were different units of length for different yarns, e.g. cotton, wool, and jute and, in the wool trade, different locations.

Dram or tram. A wheeled tub for conveying coal at the colliery.

Duff coal. Small coal unsuitable for retail sale. Used for firing boilers at collieries.

Economiser. A system of pre-heating boiler feed-water, using the heat of the waste gases in the boiler flues. First invented in 1843 by Edward Green of Wakefield, Yorks.

Edge tools. These were any kind of hand tool with a sharp cutting edge, such as a spade, hoe, sickle or scythe. A strip of toughened steel was forged as a sandwich between softer metal, and then sharpened. This was an ancient craft, some of the sites utilising water-powered tilt hammers.

Egg-ended boiler. A horizontal cylindrical boiler with hemispherical ends and no flues. At early pattern, superseded by the Cornish and Lancashire types.

Flitches. The two halves of the beam of a beam engine. Originally cast solid, beams were sometimes made in two halves and kept apart by spacers and bolts.

Glands. These were recessed bosses in the cylinder cover or valve chest of a steam engine or pump which were fitted with fibre or metal packing. They allowed the rods to work freely without leaking steam or water.

Governor. This device controlled the speed of the engine, if it was too fast or too slow, by regulating the steam supply. There were many patterns but all depended on rotating weights which adjusted the control mechanism.

Grid. The National Grid, the national electricity supply system, was begun in the 1920's. Before it became very widespread by the 1950's, many small towns and larger businesses generated their own supplies, with varying supply standards.

Hoppit or hoppet. A large basket used in mining.

Lodge. A pond located near a mill's engine-house which held the engine's condensing water. More common where the site was not previously water powered.

Manhattan engine. This was a design which coupled a horizontal and a vertical engine driving to the same crank pin. The idea surfaced around 1870 and reached its zenith in the engines driving the Manhattan (New York) power stations in the early 1900's. A number were made by various makers for use in Britain, driving textile mills, rolling mills and London Tramways power generation.

McNaughting was patented by William McNaught of Glasgow in 1845. Piston loads were thus opposed, so reducing stresses on the beam centre. The fitting of high pressure boilers and compound working gave great economy.

Mule. Cotton spinning machine, invented by Crompton, so named because it incorporated the roller-drawing principle of Arkwright's water frame and the carriage drawing of Hargreave's spinning jenny. The first successful self-acting mule was invented by Richard Roberts 1830.

Non-dead centre engines. These were vertical or horizontal engines in which two parallel cylinders were coupled to a single crank pin by a triangular connecting rod, and had the advantage of starting at almost any crank position. Twin or quadruple cylinder compound engines were common. Their heyday was 1880-1907.

Northrop loom. An automatic loom invented by 1894 by J. H. Northrop in the USA.

Overwinding gear. This was an apparatus to stop a winding engine lifting a cage beyond the pit bank and damaging itself and contents on the pit frame. Various systems were used.

Process steam. This was steam after it had left the engine and before it was condensed. It was used in the plant for other purposes such as central heating, heating dye vats, drying paper.

Rastrick Boiler. A pattern of vertical boiler which utilised the waste heat from wrought iron-making processes.

Ring spinning. A system where the spinning spindle revolves within a ring, with a small steel hoop on the flange of the ring to govern the winding-on of the thread.

Room and Power. The term means that a capitalist established a factory with a power supply (usually steam), and heating, and rented out space to small craftsmen or manufacturers. Each floor had a drive shaft taken from the engine from which individual machines, owned and worked by the tenants, were driven.

Shear. Mechanical scissors used for cropping billets of steel during the rolling process.

Sizing. The stiffening of fabrics with various pastes or starches.

Slow banking. This involved the means of controlling the winding engine carefully to allow precise location of the cage at the finish of the wind.

Tentering or stentering. This was the action of stretching cloth whilst drying to ensure all the threads were in line. Originally done by hand, latterly by machine.

Sources
Definitions and illustrations used have been drawn from:

Wilfred Lineham, *A text book of Mechanical Engineering*, 9ed, 1906.

Arnold Lupton, *Mining*, 3ed, 1906.

William S. Murphy, The *Textile Industries*, 8 vol, 1910.

Herman Haeder and H. H. P. Powles, *Handbook on the Steam Engine*, 4ed, 1914.

More detailed technical information about engine design may be found in:

Colin Bowden, 'The stationary steam engine: a critical bibliography', Industrial Archaeology Review, XV, (1992-3), pp 177-194.

George Watkins, *The Stationary Steam Engine*, 1968.

George Watkins, *The Textile Mill Engine*, 2 vol, 1970, 1971 (reprinted Landmark Publications, 1 vol, 1999).

George Watkins, & R. A. Buchanan, *Man and the Steam Engine*, 1975, 2ed 1978.

R. A. Buchanan & George Watkins, *The Industrial Archaeology of the Stationary Steam Engine*, (1976) This is a very authoritative account of the evolution of design and construction.

George Watkins. *The Steam Engine in Industry*, 2 vol, (1978, 1978). The linking passages describing the application of steam to different industries are specially valuable.

Transactions of the Newcomen Society, especially:

Arnold Throp 'Some notes on the history of the Uniflow Steam Engine', vol 43 (1970-71) pp 19-39.

George Watkins, 'The development of the Steam Winding Engine' vol 50, (1978-79), pp 11-24.

James L. Wood, 'The introduction of the Corliss Engine into Britain', vol 52, (1980-81) pp 1-13.

R. L. Hills, 'The Uniflow engine, a re-appraisal' Vol 57, (1985-6) , pp 59-77.

R. W. M. Clouston, 'The development of the Babcock Boiler in Britain up to 1939', vol 58, (1986-87), pp 75-87.

James L. Wood. 'The Sulzer steam engine comes to Britain', vol 59, (1987-88), pp 129-152.

Stationary Power (The Journal of the International Steam Engine Society), especially:

William D. Sawyer, Corliss Man and engine, 2 vol, 1994, (JISSES 10), 1997, (JISSES 13)

1. Accrington, Huncoat Colliery   SER 1338

Type:	Horizontal double cylinder
Photo taken:	1968
Maker and Date:	Daglish & Co., St. Helens, 1890
Cylinder/dimensions:	26in x 5ft 0in – Cornish valves
Hp: ?	*Rpm: 50* *Psi: 80*
Service:	Coal winding. Shaft 300 yards deep. 32 cwt coal per wind.

Very little altered in over 70 years working, this for most of its life wound 84cwt. tubs of coal on two decks, until 1954 when it was altered to use a single 3 ton mine car per wind, for which the stiffeners can be seen beside the original cast iron spider. The colliery ran thus for some 15 years when with the lower quality of the coal, and largely worked-out reserves, it was too uneconomic to run; with closure, all was scrapped. This colliery, as with some others in the Burnley area, discharged the exhaust steam into the chimney. The four boilers were used when there was a steam driven air compressor, but newer boilers from another pit were installed in the changes of the mid-1950s. The coal tubs were moved by compressed air-driven rams; the air decking system greatly speeded tub changes in banking or landing the coal at top and bottom of the pit.

2. Ashton-under-Lyne, Cedar Mill, Hurst   SER 1064

Type:	Inverted vertical triple expansion
Photo taken:	1961
Maker and Date:	George Saxon Ltd., Manchester, 1905
Cylinder/dimensions:	22.$^1/_2$in – 32in and 50in x 4ft 0in
Hp: 1,200	*Rpm: 75* *Psi: 160*
Service:	Cotton spinning, 28 ropes to drive 5 floors. 22ft 0in flywheel.

A standard Saxons vertical triple in the usual small engine room of the later vertical engine period of the early 1900s, which was the last great expansion era of the English cotton trade. Four hand-fired Oldham Boiler Works boilers were installed for 180 psi originally, and they still carried this pressure nearly 60 years later. Built for mule spinning, the machinery was gradually changed over to ring frames, with an alternator to generate electrically the current, but by 1965 the engine load was reduced to some 400 hp, and the whole was put on to the Grid, and the engine was scrapped. The ropes fitted at Cedar indicate the division of the load in a spinning mill, and of the 27 ropes to drive the entire mill, 12 were fitted to drive the preparation section on the bottom floor where the carding engines, and openers and breakers were placed. The engine at Cedar Mill was unusually close to the mill shafts, only about 27 ft between centres for the bottom drives. The mill remained at work until the mid 1960s.

3. Ashton-under-Lyne, Gartsides Ltd, Wellington Mills   SER 807

Type:	Inverted vertical triple expansion
Photo taken:	
Maker and Date:	Scott & Hodgson, Guide Bridge, c.1903
Cylinder/dimensions:	22in – 37in – 62in x 4ft 6in
Hp: 2000	*Rpm: 78* *Psi: 160*
Service:	Cotton spinning, rope drive.

This was a typical Scott & Hodgson design with the very slight connecting rods, and as usual gave little trouble although heavily loaded. There were two piston valves to the low and one on the intermediate cylinders, a frequent Scott & Hodgson feature for large powers. Later, part of the load was taken electrically from an alternator driven by ropes from the engine, and the whole mill went to electric driving from the Grid about 1953, and was possibly closed in the reorganisation of 1960.

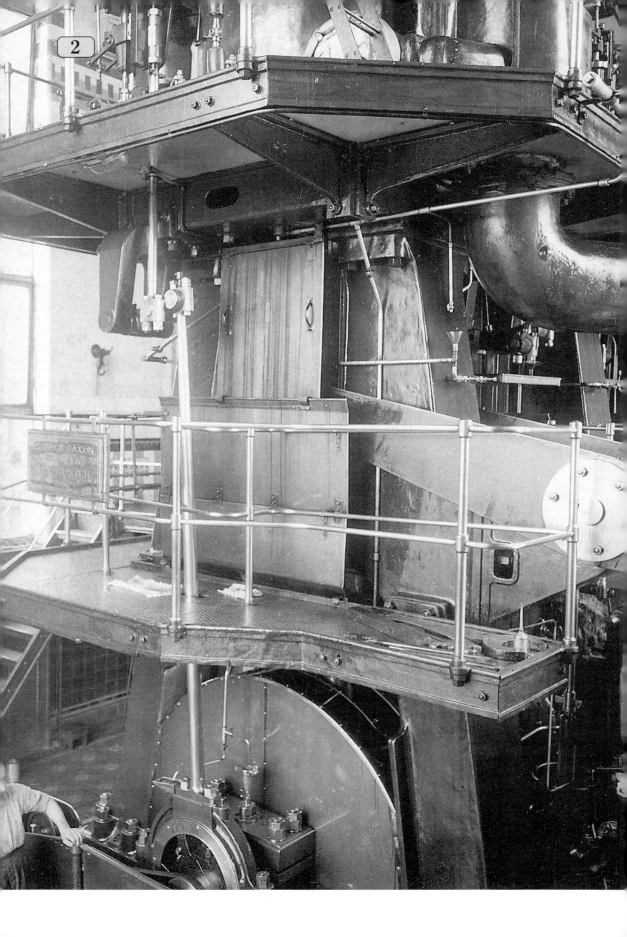

4. Atherton, The Howe Bridge Spinning Co., No 3 Mill   SER 756 (3)

Type: Horizontal cross compound condensing
Photo taken: 1955
Maker and Date: John Musgrave & Sons, Bolton, 1889
Cylinder/dimensions: 30in and 60in x 7ft 0in – Corliss valves
Hp: Approx. 2,000   *Rpm:* 54   *Psi:* 160
Service: Cotton spinning. 34 ropes. Flywheel 34ft 0in diameter.

This was the largest flywheel in a Lancashire mill although there may have been one of 36ft diameter in Scotland. The engine ran for some seventy years with virtually no alteration, except possibly for a new high pressure cylinder when the boilers were renewed. It was a splendid engine yet very simple, retaining the original governors unaltered, and the pressure and vacuum gauge panel seen near to the barring engine was probably the least pretentious of any for a large engine. With the re-equipment of the mills, two buildings were superfluous and were demolished, and the ground sold.

5. Atherton, Howe Bridge Colliery   SER 757

Type: Four coupled locomotive
Photo taken: 1955
Maker and Date: Hawthorn & Co., Leith, 1861
Cylinder/dimensions:
Hp: *Rpm:*   *Psi:*
Service: Colliery yard haulage.

This was Davidson's patent design in which the main framing comprised the boiler feed water tanks, with the motion attached to plates fitted to the sides of the tanks, and with the axles in front and behind the tank frame. This made it impossible to fit the valve gearing inside the frame in the usual manner and it was therefore fitted outside the coupling rods, and driven from a crank on the driving crankpin.

6. Atherton, Laburnum Spinning Co., No. 1 Mill   SER 715

Type: Horizontal – four cylinder triple expansion
Photo taken:
Maker and Date: John & Edward Wood, Bolton, 1905
Cylinder/dimensions: 24in–36in–40in and 40ft x 5'0in – Corliss valves
Hp: 1800   *Rpm:* 70   *Psi:* 180
Service: Cotton Spinning

Named *Capital* and *Labour*, this was a very fine example of a Wood engine in an equally fine engine room. The No.2. mill was a little later and was always driven by electric motors. No 1 mill was changed over to electrically driven ring frames in the 1960s, and only boiler capacity for mill heating was retained.

4

6

7. Atherton, St. Georges Colliery   SER 1007

Type:	Horizontal twin cylinder non-condensing
Photo taken:	1959
Maker and Date:	John Musgrave & Sons, Bolton
Cylinder/dimensions:	32in x 5ft 0in – Cornish valves
Hp: ?	*Rpm:* 30 *Psi:* 100
Service:	No. 1 shaft. Coal winding.

This was an old pit that was nearly worked out, and producing little coal in the 1950s. There was also a Worsley Mesnes engine of similar design for No. 2 shaft, with 11 boilers of various makes steaming the air compressors and other plant. The pumps had long been electrically driven, and, latterly, so was the fan. It was a typical small colliery of the later 19th century, which had been well maintained. The winding engine was a typical Musgrave early winding engine design, with the four valves in the corners of the cylinders, and latterly automatic trip cut-off had been fitted to the inlet valves. There was no exhaust steam turbine system, but there was a small power-station for the lighting and small auxilliary electrical load. The pit was finally closed and all scrapped in the early 1960s.

8. Bacup, Forest Mill   SER 155

Type:	Double beam cross compounded
Photo taken:	1935
Maker and Date:	Unknown
Cylinder/dimensions:	18in and 36in x 6ft 0in – Corliss HP, slide valve LP
Hp: 100?	*Rpm:* 90 *Psi:* ?
Service:	Cotton weaving. Gear drive off rim. 2 pinions for mill and shed drives. Beam 21ft 0in long. Flywheel 21ft 0in diameter.

No record remained of this engine, or by whom it was made, or when the conversion to cross compound was made. The Whitehead Corliss gear suggests that it could be in the late 1890s, but the engine had been greatly altered, possibly when a connecting rod or crank failed, since the high pressure side had a forged steel connecting rod, with the original cast iron one on the low pressure side. The teeth on the flywheel rim had been renewed and these gave much trouble, but this could well have been due to changing the weaving shed drive from gears to ropes; the sway of the ropes always caused backlash on the main drive gearing.

9. Bacup, Wm. Greaves & Co., The Sizing House   SER 1102

Type:	Horizontal single tandem
Photo taken:	1962
Maker and Date:	Unknown, c.1888? (date on mill front)
Cylinder/dimensions:	9in and 18in x 2ft 0in – Slide valves
Hp: 60	*Rpm:* 90 *Psi:* 100
Service:	Plant for dressing yarn with size for the weaving trade.

The history of the plant was confused, and the engine room and the drives certainly suggested that it may once have been a weaving shed, with a beam engine or gear drive. The flat planed cross-head guide surface, the disc crank, and the condenser placed beside the crank were all unusual features for a mill, and the engine may have been secondhand from another place. The main drive was from the flywheel to the mill shaft by a leather belt some 9in wide. The plant closed in the cotton trade re-organisations of the 1960s, since man-made fibres are not treated with size.

7

9

10. Bacup, Joshua Hoyle & Co., India Mill   SER 154

Type:	Double McNaughted beam
Photo taken:	1935
Maker and Date:	J. Petrie & Co., Rochdale, 1860s?
Cylinder/dimensions:	Built as twin 40in x 7ft 0in? –Slide valves
	Tripled by Yates & Thom.? – Corliss valves HP
Hp: 1200	*Rpm:* 25 *Psi:* 175
Service:	Cotton spinning and doubling. Gear drive off flywheel arms. Beam 22ft 6in long. Flywheel 24ft 0in diameter. Electric drive after breakdown in 1951.

Typical Petrie engine: very heavy build, with massive flywheel, and drive taken from a single pinion to the vertical shaft. The high pressure cylinder was mahogany-lagged. It would not have been scrapped, but for the breakdown.

11. Bacup, Rossendale Industrial Co-operative   SER 153

Type:	Double McNaughted beam
Photo taken:	1935
Maker and Date:	Wood Bros., Sowerby Bridge, 1863
Cylinder/dimensions:	No cylinder sizes – 6ft crank stroke
Hp: 500	*Rpm:* 20 *Psi:* 80?
Service:	Cotton spinning. Gear drive off flywheel rim by one 6ft 0in pinion. Beam 20ft 0in long. Flywheel 20ft 0in diameter. Scrapped 1938.

Built by Wood Bros. and McNaughted by them in the 1890s, this was largely as built. The LP cylinders retained the 4 slide valves per cylinder, all of which worked across the valve chest face, from a vertical cam shaft. The cut-off varied by a handwheel at the top of the camshaft. The HP cylinder had plain slide valves only. There were 4 Lancashire boilers, with bricked up fronts, working at 80 psi, which also steamed the weaving shed engine, a plain slide valve cross-compound horizontal. Weaving stopped about 1940.

12. Bacup, H. W. Trickett   SER 1147

Type:	Horizontal single tandem
Photo taken:	1964
Maker and Date:	Wm. Sharples, Ramsbottom, No. 677, 1900
Cylinder/dimensions:	14in and 26in x 2ft 6in – Slide valves
Hp: 200	*Rpm:* 102 *Psi:* 130
Service:	Mill drive. 6 ropes to mill and 3 to alternator. Slipper manufacturers

Named *Janie* (HP) and *Elsie* (LP) this was probably the last small Sharples engine at work, and certainly the last with slide valves. The speed control was by variable cut-off from a sliding valve on the back of the high pressure slide valve, under the control of a shaft governor. The mill was cotton spinning until 1900, with a beam engine and gears. The tandem engine was then installed, on the change of business, in a new engine house at the lower end of the mill. The drives were mixed, first by ropes from the engine to the alternator and mill mainshaft, and then by belts to the upper floors. The whole of the drives were to be converted to electric motors in the early 1960s, using current from the Grid, and the engine was to be scrapped.

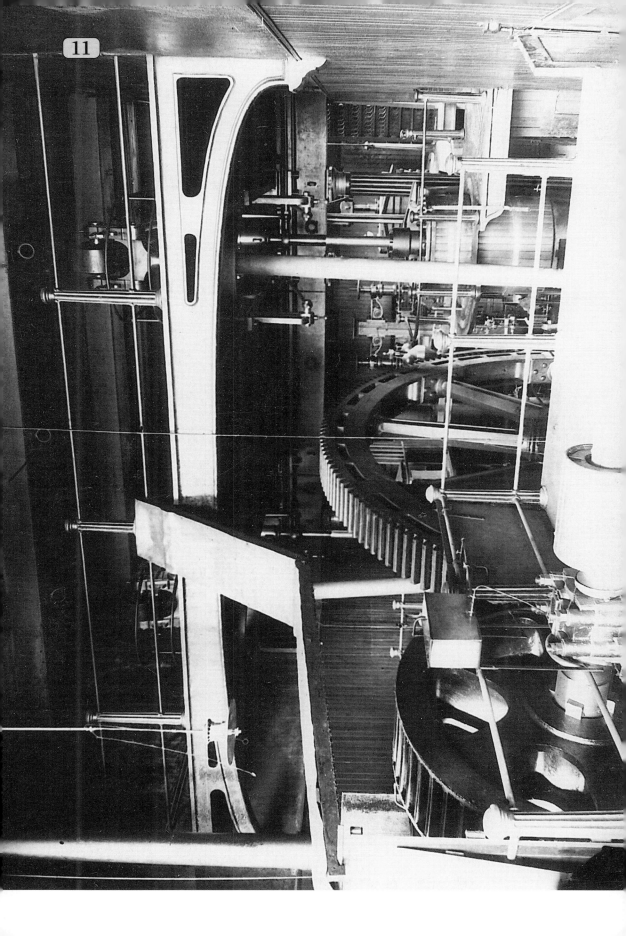

13. Barrow in Furness, The Barrow Haematite Steel Works   SER 988

Type:	Horizontal twin cylinder non-condensing
Photo taken:	1959
Maker and Date:	Davy Bros., Sheffield, 1894
Cylinder/dimensions:	50in x 4ft 6in – Slide valves
Hp: 3,000	Rpm: 120 Psi: 120
Service:	Direct drive to steel rolling mill.

The roughing and the finishing mills each had a similar engine, rolling ingots to 2in x 2in bars for the re-rollers. A small balance wheel was fitted between the cranks, and the engines were interesting in having double-webbed cranks whereas many Davy twin engines had half cranks with no outer bearing. The works was developing a direct casting system, by which the 2in x 2in bar was directly moulded from the ladle which would supersede the rolling process. The blast furnaces at the works were blown out in the early 1960s, when supplies of waste gas for steam making ceased, and the boilers were oil-fuel fired. The works was closed and all was scrapped in the later steel trade re-organisation of the 1970s.

14. Barrowford, nr. Nelson, Atkinson Ltd., Lower Clough Mill SER 979

Type:	Horizontal cross compound
Photo taken:	1959
Maker and Date:	Wm. Roberts & Sons, Phoenix Foundry, Nelson, 1889
Cylinder/dimensions:	24in and 42in x 5ft 0in – Slide valves
Hp: 800	*Rpm:* 54 *Psi:* 110
Service:	Cotton weaving. Gear drive.

This remained unaltered until automatic looms and motor drives were installed about 1960-1961. It retained the Roberts design of placing the high pressure cylinder slide valves on the outer side of the cylinder, with a cross cut-off valve under governor control, and there was no record of any changes in the two boilers; it seems likely that the original ones ran the engine for its life of some 70 years. It certainly ran well until, with the plant changes, it was scrapped together with the shaft drives in the shed. The photograph was taken when it was running.

15. Baxenden, nr. Accrington, Nicholas Worsley & Co.   SER 883

Type:	Horizontal cross compound condensing
Photo taken:	1957
Maker and Date:	C. Whittaker & Co., Haslingden, 1908
Cylinder/dimensions:	19in and 36in x 4ft 0in – Corliss and piston valves
Hp: 750	*Rpm:* 75 *Psi:* 150
Service:	Textile finishing. 15 rope drive.

Whittaker & Co were best known for their brickmaking machinery, but the few engines that they built gave very good service, and were of plain and substantial design. This engine was very well finished, and well kept. There were forged bosses on the middle of the valve and engine connecting rods. It was unusual to place a pinch-barring rack upon the face of the barring engine crankface, as seen on the print. The low pressure cylinder was fitted with a piston valve with twist cut-off motion, operated by a feather on the valve spindle guide, similar to that of Petrie. It was regrettable that this well-kept plant was scrapped when electric drives were adopted in 1958-9.

14

16. Blackburn, Clayton St. Mills   SER 783

Type:	Horizontal cross compound condensing
Photo taken:	1956
Maker and Date:	Clayton, Goodfellow, Blackburn, No. 422-423, 1894
Cylinder/dimensions:	14.$^1/_2$in and 29in x 3ft 6in – Corliss and slide valves
Hp: 165	*Rpm:* 61 *Psi:* 120
Service:	Cotton cloth weaving. Geared drive off flywheel arms.

This was probably a new engine replacing a beam engine which was damaged in a fire. There was very little room around it and the beam engine was probably twin cylinder type. The high pressure side was named *Success* and the low pressure *Progress*. It was unusual for Clayton, Goodfellow to have single slipper crosshead guides as here, and it is possible that it was in fact a secondhand engine which they overhauled, and fitted with a new high pressure cylinder, and new boiler to start production rapidly after the fire. It was a very plain and simple engine with no characteristics to suggest a possible maker, but the high pressure cylinder was certainly Clayton, Goodfellow.

17. Blackburn, Eastwoods Ltd., Scotland Bank Mill   SER 882

Type:	Horizontal single tandem condensing
Photo taken:	1957
Maker and Date:	Ashton, Frost & Co., Blackburn, 1911
Cylinder/dimensions:	15in and 30in x 3ft 0in – Drop valves
Hp: 400	*Rpm:* 90 *Psi:* 160
Service:	Weaving shed. Direct drive from crankshaft, by coupling.

This was the only engine of the design that Ashton, Frost & Co made, and was unusual in that the drop valves were at one side of the cylinder, not, as usual on the top, and were driven by the usual side layshaft. This engine was also unusual for Ashton, Frost as it had a mammoth type trunk frame, whereas they usually adopted the twin slipper type. It appeared to be the work of a new designer following the trend toward drop valves and higher pressures and superheat, which developed when high economy was secured from such engines on the Continent. It ran very well, despite some trouble from misalignment at the start, the engine being coupled directly to the mill mainshaft.

18. Blackburn, E. & G. Hindle Ltd., Bastfield Mill   SER 985a

Type:	Horizontal cross compound
Photo taken:	1959
Maker and Date:	Wm. & Jno. Yates, Blackburn, c.1870s?
Cylinder/dimensions:	20$^1/_2$ in and 34$^1/_2$ in x 4ft 0in – Slide valves
Hp: 700	*Rpm:* 48$^1/_2$ *Psi:* 130
Service:	Cotton weaving. Gear drive off flywheel rim.

This was probably built as a simple expansion twin cylinder in the 1870s, and a new high pressure cylinder by Clayton, Goodfellow was fitted in the early 1880s. There had certainly been many alterations in its lifetime, but it kept a prosperous business going for nearly a century, until the mill was closed in the Cotton Spindle Redundancy Scheme in 1961, when mills were closed on Government payments for the plant. There had certainly been a new flywheel, and the left hand side had a new cylinder which was totally different from Yates' practice, but the engine motion was characteristic of Yates' design. The right hand side appeared to have had a new crosshead guiding system. The speed governor was on the weaving shed drive shaft, not driven off the engine, as was usually done. The high pressure cylinder valve gear was unusual, in that Clayton, Goodfellow's Corliss trip motion was fitted to operate the cross cut-off slide valves on the back of the main valve. An interesting unit with all of the work of local craftsmanship. Part of the load was by an alternator fitted in 1929 to drive new automatic looms, still in use in the 1950s.

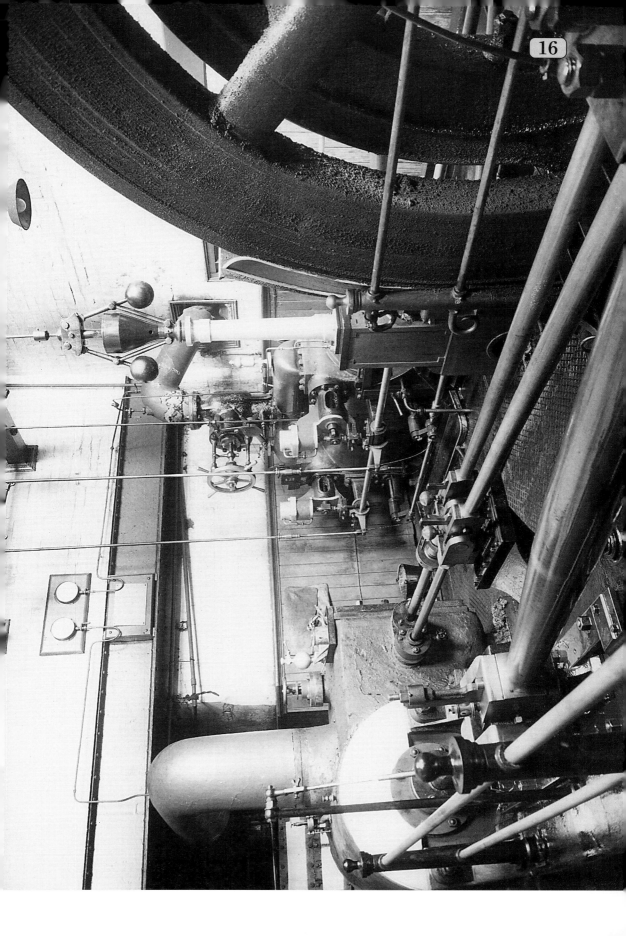

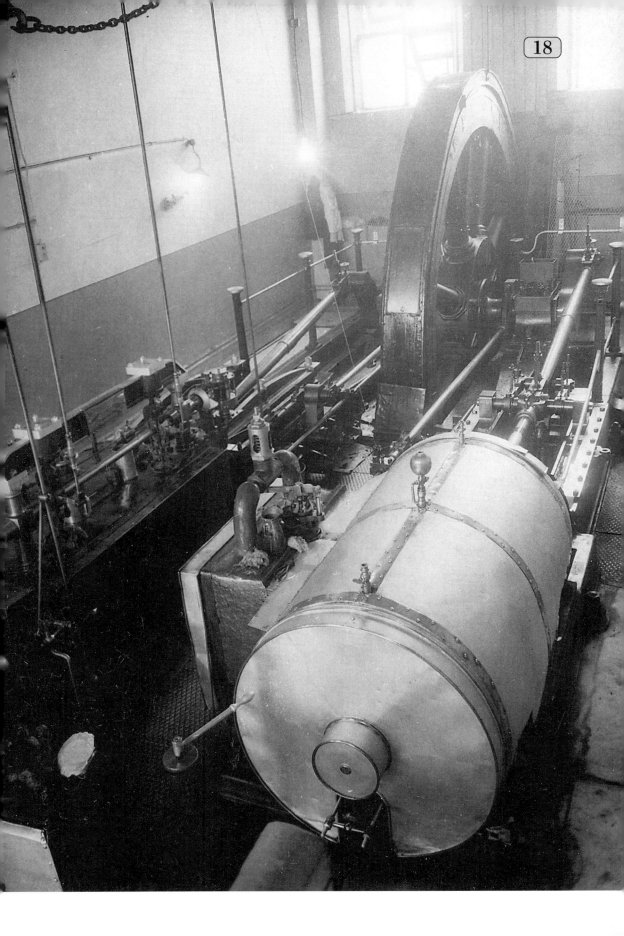

19. Blackburn, E. & G. Hindle Ltd., Bastfield Mill   SER 985b

Type:	Vertical single cylinder non-condensing
Photo taken:	1959
Maker and Date:	B. Goodfellow, Hyde, No. 78, 1851
Hp: Approx. 10	*Rpm:* 90 *Psi:* 130

This was used to drive the fitting shop machinery when the weaving shed was stopped, the usual drive being from the shed mainshaft. It was unaltered, and, plain and simple, never had much repair. Largely fitting and blacksmith work, it was a pleasing reminder of the early simple engine designs which did all that they were designed for. The history of the engine was uncertain, it was doubtful if the business was as old as 1851, yet it seemed a part of the plant that was original. It was purchased by an unknown buyer for preservation when the plant was closed. Certainly at the time it was the oldest small engine in regular use, as it was used at weekends in the 1950s.

20. Blackburn, E. & G. Hindle Ltd., Swallow Street Mill   SER 1022

Type:	Horizontal cross compound
Photo taken:	1960
Maker and Date:	W. & J. Yates, 1874
Cylinder/dimensions:	26in and 46in x 6ft 6in as rebuilt
Hp: 700	*Rpm:* 45 *Psi:* 120
Service:	Cotton weaving. 1400 looms. Geared drive.

The plant consisted of three weaving sheds, all driven by gearing from the one engine. It was almost certainly built as a twin slide-valve engine, possibly about 30in x 6ft 6in cylinders with the 1,000 loom main shed in 1874, and three boilers. The boiler plant was ageing by 1904 and more power was needed, so new boilers and a Corliss valve high pressure cylinder was put in by Ashton, Frost; the other cylinder was replaced by a Yates & Thom Corliss valve one, possibly in the 1920s. A new shed had also been added and the plant ran economically in this way until 1952, when electrical drives were installed. The plant then only ran until 1960, when it was all scrapped under the Cotton Spindle Reduction Scheme. It had long been a good business.

21. Blackburn, M. Munro & Son, Guide   SER 830

Type:	Horizontal cross compound
Photo taken:	
Maker and Date:	Ashton, Frost and Co., Bank Top Foundry, Blackburn
Cylinder/dimensions:	17in and 30in x 3ft 6in – Corliss and slide valves
Hp: 500	*Rpm:* 84 *Psi:* 160
Service:	Cotton Weaving. 12 rope drive to Two Sheds

The business was old but possibly taken over by another company and this engine was installed to drive the existing and a new shed then erected, possibly in the early 1900s. It was extremely well kept even when idle, but the whole was sold for scrap when the business was closed in 1958. Although there were suggestions of Shorrocks make in it, Ashton, Frost were probably the makers' by insurance records. The rope drive went back over the engine to a countershaft from which a drive then went forward to the original shed with a bevel wheel driving the new shed off the other end of the counter shaft.

19

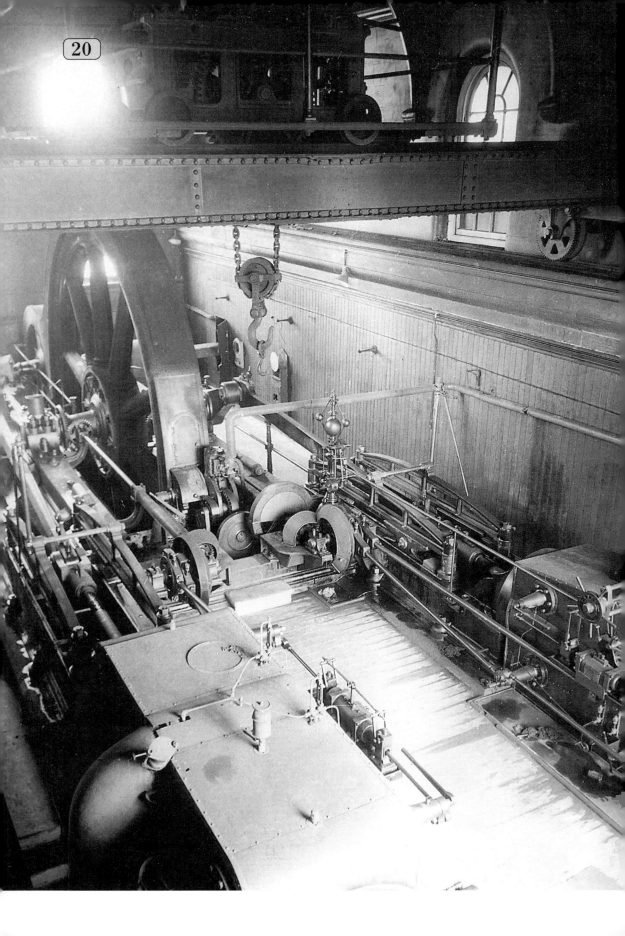

21

22. Blackburn, The Scrim Manufacturing Co., Hollinshead Mill   SER 902

Type:	Horizontal single tandem
Photo taken:	1958
Maker and Date:	Ashton, Frost & Co., Blackburn, 1906
Cylinder/dimensions:	15in and 30in x 2ft 6in – Corliss and slide valves
Hp: 400	*Rpm:* 90 *Psi:* 160
Service:	Cotton weaving. Direct drive to weaving shed mainshaft.

This was a typical Ashton, Frost & Co smaller engine design; neat and strong and which had been well maintained with very little altered. The whole engine was raised some 9 feet above the mill level to allow it to be connected to the mill mainshaft, from which the looms were driven by 11 bevel driven cross shafts. The governor was unaltered as indeed was the whole engine, which also had the Blackburn area feature: namely that the boiler feed pump was driven from the low pressure cylinder slide valvetail-rod. The exhaust steam was frequently taken to the condenser by an overhead pipe from the low pressure cylinder which simplified the foundation plinth as it eliminated the underground piping. The condition of the engine was typical of a small but keen company, with a good engineer. The mill was closed and the whole was scrapped about 1958.

23. Blackburn, Vernon and Co., Columbia Mill   SER 781

Type:	Horizontal cross compound condensing
Photo taken:	1956
Maker and Date:	Clayton, Goodfellow, Blackburn, c.1870?
Cylinder/dimensions:	18in and 36in x 4ft 0in – Corliss and slide valves
Hp: 350	*Rpm:* 45 *Psi:* 100
Service:	Cotton cloth weaving. Gear drive off flywheel rim.

This was probably an early Clayton, Goodfellow engine, being very similar to that at Victoria Mill (SER828). Probably built as a twin cylinder engine, it was altered to compound by replacing the left hand cylinder by a Corliss valve as seen in the print. It was certainly typical of their earlier design, with the Blackburn feature of driving the boiler feed pump from the low pressure slide valvetail-rod. Other than metallic packings for the piston and valve rods, little was altered and the original governor was retained until, with the trade re-organisation, the mill was believed to have closed when all was scrapped. The toothed flywheel rim drove directly to the pinion on the shed side shaft, with the usual belt drives to the looms and the sizing plant for the warp yarn.

24. Blackburn, Victoria Mill, Hall Street   SER 828

Type:	Horizontal cross compound
Photo taken:	1956
Maker and Date:	Clayton, Goodfellow, Blackburn, No. 137-8, 1869
Cylinder/dimensions:	18in and 33in x 5ft 0in – Slide valves
Hp: Approx. 240	*Rpm:* 36 *Psi:* 80
Service:	Cotton weaving. Gear drive.

This was almost certainly built as a twin cylinder engine, and altered possibly in the 1890s, by the fitting of a new high pressure cylinder and higher pressure boiler. It is probable that originally the cylinders were the same as that seen on the left. The high pressure cylinder was fitted with a Meyer cut-off valve with manual adjustment. But for the cylinder, and the fitting of a high speed governor, the engine was virtually as built. It always ran very well, the gear drive being especially quiet. The mill closed and all was scrapped in 1958.

25. Bolton, Barlow and Jones, Albert Mill, Bridge Street   SER 856a

Type: Horizontal cross compound condensing
Photo taken: 1957
Maker and Date: Hick, Hargreaves and Co., Bolton, 1913
Cylinder/dimensions: 26in and 52in x 4ft 0in – Corliss valves
Hp: 2,300   *Rpm:* 84   *Psi:* 175
Service: Cotton spinning by 19 ropes, and alternator.

This concern had 8 engines in their various mills, and this was the largest and latest of their Corliss engines, since afterwards they adopted uniflow engines for their last two. This was a massive fine engine that had long been heavily loaded, taking up to 850 hp on the ropes and over 1250 kW on the alternator. It was a late example of fitting the alternator directly on to the crankshaft, and the combined driving system gave flexibilty with the electrical load. All of the engines were, however, scrapped in a very costly electrical conversion scheme in the 1960s, and the business was still active in 1972.

26. Bolton, Bee Hive Spinning Co.   SER 855

Type: Horizontal twin tandem triple expansion
Photo taken: 1957
Maker and Date: Hick, Hargreaves & Co., Bolton, 1903
Cylinder/dimensions: 25in – 39in – 42in x 5ft 0in – Corliss valves
Hp: 2,000   *Rpm:* 72   *Psi:* 200
Service: Cotton spinning. 43 rope drive.

This, identical almost with the No.1 mill engine, was interesting in having the earlier Spencer Inglis type trip gear rather than the lighter crab-claw type that Hicks were then using. The engines had given exceptional service, and were unaltered when No.1 mill was closed about 1956. The load on No.2 was less than half the designed amount by 1962. Cotton spinning was probably abandoned in the late 1960s, but in the confused trade conditions a positive record was impossible to discover. Almost all of the machinery was always scrapped. In 1914 the two mills contained 262,000 mule spinning spindles, using over 4,000 hp, on two engines and two boiler plants with four boilers in each, and about 600 employees in all.

27. Bolton, Thos. Crook & Co., Engineers, Derby Street   SER 1403

Type: Horizontal single cylinder non-condensing
Photo taken: 1970
Maker and Date: Thos. Crook, Bolton, 1860s?
Cylinder/dimensions: 12in x 1ft 9in – Slide valve
Hp: Approx. 25   *Rpm:* 85   *Psi:* 70
Service: Drove engineers' works plant by 8in belt.

The works were started as general engineers, and developed a good business in making mortar-mixing pans, brickmaking machinery, and asphalt mixers, as well as a wide range of general engineering work. They made many small steam engines and a speciality was mortar- mixing pans with the engine combined, steam being supplied by a separate vertical boiler and the engines having pitchfork connecting rods. The little works engine which was on a floor above the boiler was typical of their work, plain simple and trouble free and even the metallic piston-rod packing fitted later was of Crook's own make, and they supplied many sets for other engines. There was no local water supply for condensing, so the exhaust was discharged in to the air, and with no economiser all the steam was wasted, the boiler feed water being cold. There was a good foundry for the general castings, and the mortar mills, but very little casting was done after 1927. Latterly much of the machinery was newer and driven by attached electric motors. The little business was closed about 1970, when there was a staff of about 10 men.

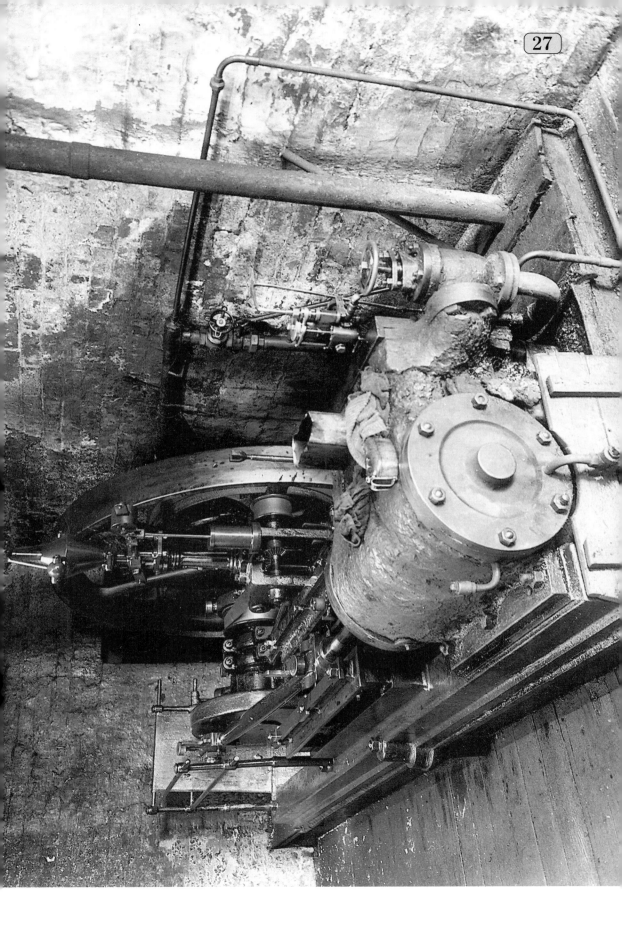

28. Bolton, Thos. Crook & Co.   SER 1403a

Type:	Vertical single cylinder non-condensing
Photo taken:	1970
Maker and Date:	Thos. Crook and Co., Bolton, Date unknown
Cylinder/dimensions:	Approx, 6in x 8in – Slide valve
Hp: 5-6	*Rpm:* 100 *Psi:* 70
Service:	Pattern Makers' loft.

The whole of the machines they sold were made on the premises, requiring many castings and a wide range of patterns was stocked: wherever possible, casting rather than fabrication was adopted. Beside the general range of mortar and brick making machines, they also made small-power mill engines, such as that at Pemberton Mill (SER 862), and patterns for the bed of such an engine can be seen upon the supports on the wall above the small vertical engine. The latter is typical of the small engines which, horizontal, diagonal or vertical, they made as stock jobs. This one had driven the patternmaker's lathes, saws and other tools of that trade, by a belt on the flywheel. All of the timber sections and gears were patterns for mortar and brickmaking machines. All were scrapped.

29. Bolton, Crosses & Winkworth, Gilnow Mill   SER 178

Type:	Double McNaughted beam
Photo taken:	
Maker and Date:	J. Musgrove & Son, Bolton 1856
Cylinder/dimensions:	Built as twin cylinder – 44ft x 7'0in New Corliss valve cylinders – 18?
Hp: 1100	*Rpm:* abt 32 *Psi:* 150?
Service:	Cotton Spinning Gear drives. Vertical shaft and bevel gears.

This was extensively rebuilt with new cylinders, flywheel, connecting rods, etc., but no record remained of when, or who did this. It was believed to be Hicks, or Yates & Thom. Overloaded before, it was still overloaded with the rebuild in the 1930s. The beams, parallel motion, etc were the original. Scrapped c. 1939.

30. Bolton, The Pike Mill, Crosses and Winkworth   SER 1021a

Type:	Horizontal single cylinder condensing
Photo taken:	1960
Maker and Date:	Hick, Hargreaves & Co., Bolton, 1890
Cylinder/dimensions:	13in x 3ft 0in – Corliss valves
Hp: 95	*Rpm:* 75 *Psi:* 85
Service:	Evening shift drive for cotton combing shed. 3 rope drive to main shaft.

Cotton districts tended to specialise in particular yarns, and Bolton did so for high-class medium-fine yarns – the Bolton count as it was termed. Much of this was combed in the preparation stages; this being a slower process and involving expensive plant, could cause a bottleneck if a mill was busy with such orders. It was therefore customary to run the combing sheds on evening shifts to keep up with combed yarns, and small engines which could be clutched in to drive the combers were provided in several of the mills. This was one of these, and they were generally similar to this, a small plain but reasonably economical unit which needed little attention. It is seen beside the mill engine at The Pike Mill. The No.3 mill also had a similar combing engine in the engine room.

31. Bolton, John Harwood & Son, Woodside Mills   SER 751 (2)

Type:	Inverted vertical enclosed compound
Photo taken:	1955
Maker and Date:	Hick, Hargreaves & Co., Bolton, c.1910?
Cylinder/dimensions:	Unknown
Hp: 700	*Rpm:* 127 *Psi:* 160
Service:	Cotton spinning. Rope drive. No. 2 Mill.

This probably replaced another engine and may have come from a power station. It was of the special quick revolution type which Hick, Hargreaves designed for direct drive of electric generators, and was forced lubricated and fully enclosed, but fitted with crab-claw Corliss releasing valve gear. It was certainly very compact for the power it developed, and drove the mill from ropes in three direction, and despite the small pulley sizes and the high speed, ropes did not apparently give serious trouble. It was scrapped with the rest of the mills and plant as with No. 1 Mill.

32. Bolton, John Harwood & Son, Woodside Mills   SER 751 (1)

Type:	Horizontal single tandem condensing
Photo taken:	1955
Maker and Date:	John Musgrave & Sons, Bolton, 1884
Cylinder/dimensions:	26in and 46in x 5ft 0in – Corliss valves
Hp: 800	*Rpm:* 59 *Psi:* 120
Service:	No. 1 mill drive.

This was 70 years old when photographed and had very little alteration, except for the Tate's automatic stop valve, metallic piston rod packings, and lubricators. It remained a typical Musgrave engine of the period until the mills were closed and all scrapped in 1959.

33. Bolton, Horrockses, Crewdson Ltd., Moses Gate   SER 857

Type:	Horizontal cross compound condensing
Photo taken:	1957
Maker and Date:	Yates & Thom, Blackburn, 1914
Cylinder/dimensions:	33in and 66in x 4ft 6in – Corliss valves
Hp: 2,400	*Rpm:* 75 *Psi:* 160
Service:	Cotton spinning and weaving. Rope drives.

It was said that Yates & Thom only made two, or possibly three engines as large as this in cross compounds. Certainly it was an extremely fine unit which gave fully loaded service for many years unaltered, and even retained the original governors. All of the drives, including the weaving shed which had its own Hick, Hargreaves engine of 1,400 hp (cross compound) were by ropes and everything was scrapped when cotton production ceased in the 1960s. The Company also had very large mills in Preston.

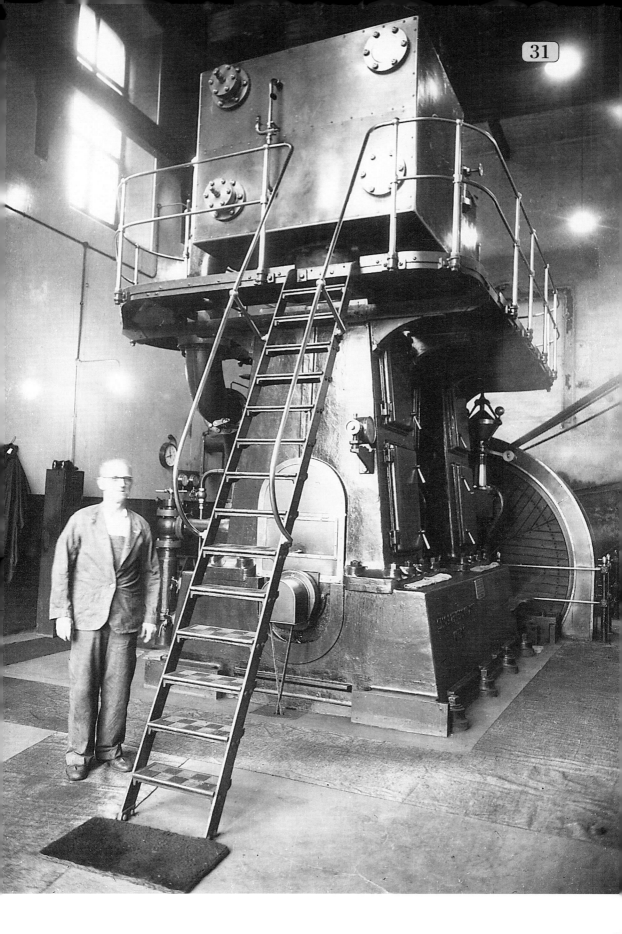

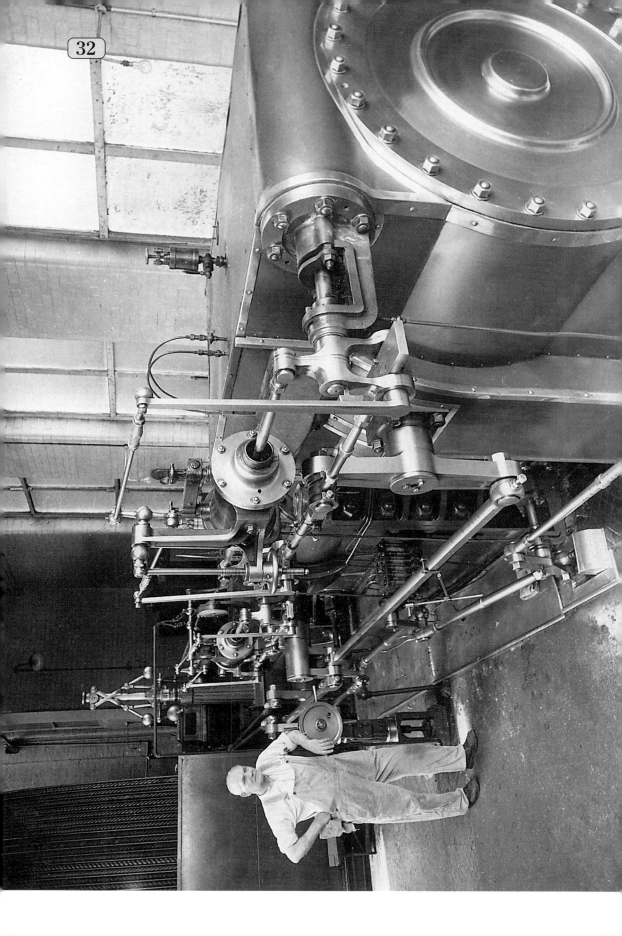

31

34. Bolton, Johnson, Hodgkinson & Pearson, Moor Mill   SER 1183

Type: Horizontal single tandem
Photo taken: 1965
Maker and Date: John Musgrave & Sons, Bolton, 1895
Cylinder/dimensions: 17in and 34in x 4ft 0in – Corliss valves
Hp: 450   *Rpm:* 75   *Psi:* 120
Service: Coarse cotton spinning. 20 rope drive to original mill shafts.

This replaced a beam engine in the same room. It was placed the opposite way to secure space for the rope drive back to the shafts of the original drive. It therefore had to run the opposite way, i.e. with the connecting rod going under on the outward stroke, and this required four-bar crosshead guides to take the upward thrust of the guide blocks. Musgrave's standard type was twin slippers, with open tops. Nothing was known of the original engine. The spinning load was quite heavy at times and the bed had a fracture at the front end, possibly due to the reverse stresses. The mill was closed and all scrapped in 1965.

35. Bolton, Joseph Johnson, Deane Shed   SER 1158

Type: Horizontal cross compound
Photo taken:
Maker and Date: J. & E. Wood. Bolton. 1907
Cylinder/dimensions: 17in and 32in x 4ft 0in – Corliss valves
Hp: 450   *Rpm:* 55   *Psi:* 160
Service: Cotton weaving. 14 ropes off 18 ft flywheel

This was a standard J. & E. Wood engine, and the only alteration had been the fitting of a Lumb governor in the 1920s, and possibly full mechanical oiling for the valve spindles. Weaving was a low cost trade, little money could be wasted, and this was the usual very plain engine room, with a glazed entry door, and lighting from the roof. The shed was re-equipped with automatic looms with the motor drives in 1965 but the engine, disused, may have remained for some years after this.

36. Bolton, Musgrave Spinning Co.   SER 725c

Type: Twin cylinder vertical single acting non-condensing
Photo taken: 1955
Maker and Date: Westinghouse Co., U. S. A., No. 361, 1887
Cylinder/dimensions: Approx. 7in x 7in – Piston valve
Hp: 20   *Rpm:* 350   *Psi:* 80
Service: Electric lighting generator.

The mills were always advanced, and this applied to electric lighting which they installed in the 1880s. This was probably a small set to provide current for the maintenance work when the main mill plant was shut down. It was probably the last of the many engines of this design which were used in U.K, but the current provided by the generator of 1897 (seen near to the engine) which replaced the original one beside the switchboard, was unsuited to the Grid specifications. It was an interesting survival of the early days, which disappeared in the modernisations.

35

36

37. *Bolton, Musgrave Spinning Co.*   *SER 833*

Type:	Single McNaught beam
Photo taken:	1956
Maker and Date:	John Musgrave & Sons, Bolton, 1868
Cylinder/dimensions:	42in x 4ft 0in and 48in x 7ft 0in – Corliss valves later
Hp: 1,000	*Rpm:* 31 *Psi:* 120
Service:	Gear drive, No. 2 Mill

The spinning side of Musgrave grew as rapidly as the engine building side, and lasted longer, to 1971 at least, and all of the engines were Musgraves. No. 1, No. 2, No. 3 and possibly No. 4 had beam engines similar to this, but No.1. Mill was closed and No.3. and No. 4 were replaced by inverted vertical compound engines with Stegen drop piston valves and superheat in 1908. Each mill had had its own boiler plant once, but latterly this was combined in one with 11 boilers. No. 2 Mill retained the beam engine until it was shut with poor trade about 1960. There were 19 boilers with 4 engines, and an electrically driven mill in 1956, with 460,00 spinning spindles. No.2 retained the vertical shaft drive always.

38. *Bolton, Musgrave Spinning Co.*   *SER 725a*

Type:	Horizontal twin tandem compound condensing
Photo taken:	1955
Maker and Date:	John Musgrave & Sons, Bolton, 1888
Cylinder/dimensions:	24in and 46in x 6ft 0in – Corliss valves
Hp: 1,750	*Rpm:* 57 *Psi:* 140
Service:	Cotton spinning. Ropedrive. No.6 Mill

The concern was a branch of the family of engine builders, and grew to a very large business, one of the largest single spinning plants in the world, with 460,000 spindles. The 1, 2, 3, and 4 Mills each had a beam engine and gear drive, and No.6. was probably the first with rope drive. It drove the No. 6 and latterly the No.7 Mill, but the original high pressure cylinders were replaced in the 1920s. No.7 was driven by a long mainshaft which passed through the cellar of No.6, and may have had a steel belt drive later. The engine was otherwise little altered until, when over 75 years old, the mill was turned to motor driving.

39. *Bolton, Musgrave Spinning Co.*   *SER 725b*

Type:	Inverted vertical compound condensing
Photo taken:	1955
Maker and Date:	John Musgrave & Sons, Bolton, 1908
Cylinder/dimensions:	33in and 65in x 4ft 0in – Drop piston valves
Hp: 3,000	*Rpm:* 75 *Psi:* 165
Service:	Cotton spinning. No. 3 Mill.

As the gearing of the No.1 to 4 mills became worn, and the engines uneconomical, they were converted to electrical driving about 1908-9 and two engines as above were installed in No.3 and 4 Mills, one of which drove No.3 by ropes as well as a generator to assist the other engine and generator. Following a cracked cylinder in 1952, one engine was stopped and later current was taken from the Grid for all of the mills, and cotton spinning continued.

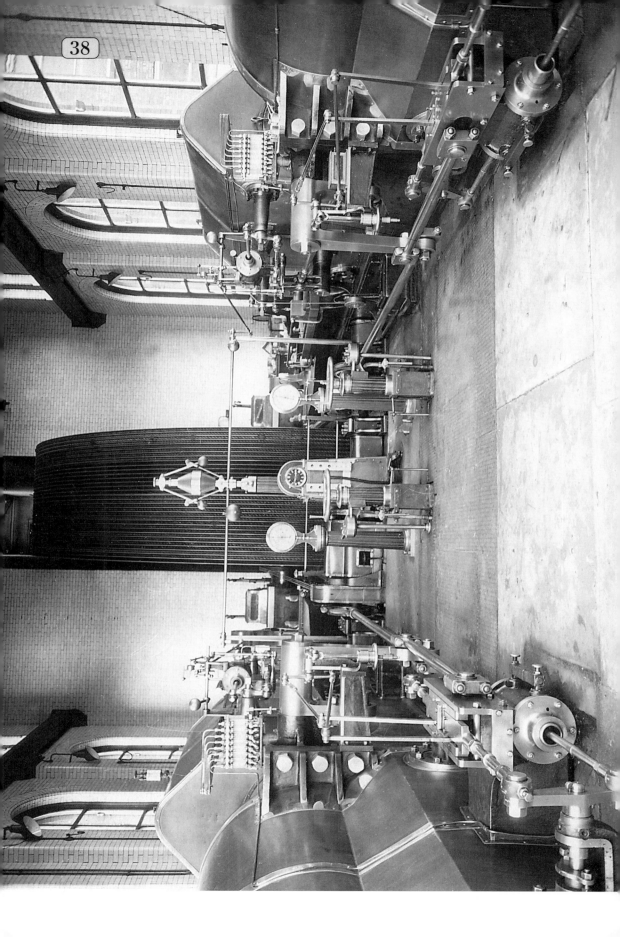

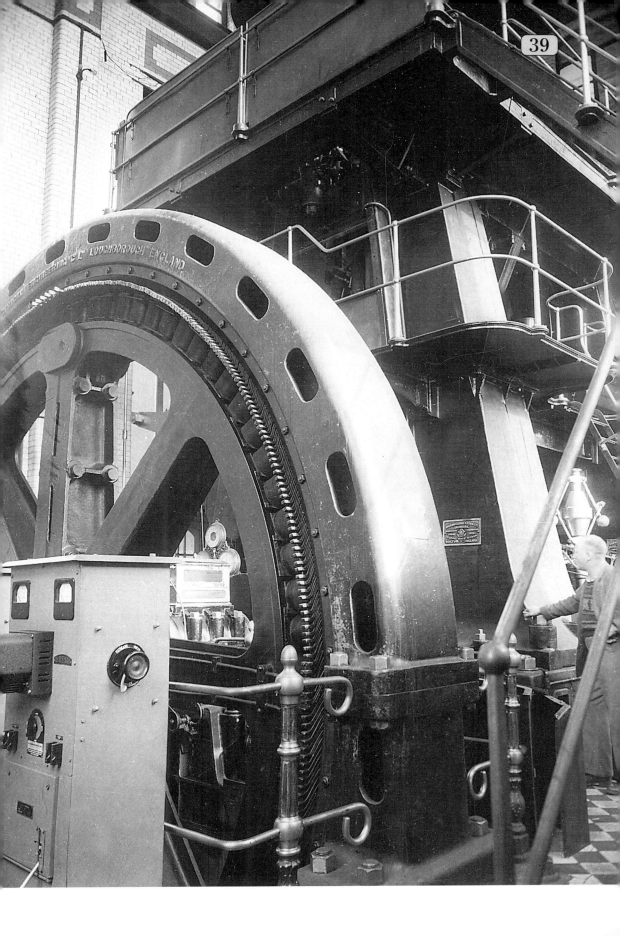

40. *Bolton, Ormrod, Hardcastle Ltd., Columbia Mill*   SER 795

Type:	Inverted vertical cross compound
Photo taken:	1956
Maker and Date:	J. & E. Wood, Bolton, 1902
Cylinder/dimensions:	18in and 36in x 4ft 0in – Corliss valves
Hp: 700	*Rpm:* 72 *Psi:* 160
Service:	Cotton spinning. Gear, later rope drive.

This was an old mill dating from the early 1870s or before, and originally had a geared drive and vertical shaft. The whole was re-arranged in 1902, when a new engine room and engine were installed to drive to the original room shafts by ropes and pulleys in an outside glass-cased rope race. It was a very effective layout, and much less noisy than the original. The mills were closed in the cotton reorganisation scheme of 1960 but the Flash St. Mill remained at work, (SER.796). The engine frames were typical of J. & E. Wood having circular holes cast in the columns, an unusual practice.

41. *Bolton, Ormrod, Hardcastle Ltd., Flash Street Mill*   SER 796

Type:	Inverted vertical triple expansion
Photo taken:	1956
Maker and Date:	Victor Coates & Co., Belfast, 1900
Cylinder/dimensions:	18in – 28in and 48in x 4ft 0in – Corliss valves
Hp: 1,000	*Rpm:* 75 *Psi:* 160
Service:	Cotton spinning. 38 rope drive.

One of the very few Irish-made engines installed in the Lancashire spinning mills, this was never loaded to more than half its designed capacity, and was replaced by electric motor drives, and the engine scrapped in 1958. It was interesting in that although there were three cast iron columns at the back of the engine frame, the centre one in the front was replaced by a forged steel vertical stay. The crankshaft was in three sections coupled by flanges between each crank, also the governing system was unusual in that the centre weight of the main governor was hollow, and there was also a supplementary governor of the Knowles type to assist it. All of the Corliss valves were across the engine centre line.

42. *Bolton, Rumworth Spinning Co.*   SER 716

Type:	Side by side horizontal compound condensing
Photo taken:	1955
Maker and Date:	Ashton, Frost & Co., Blackburn, 1901
Cylinder/dimensions:	19in and 38in x 4ft 0in – Corliss valves
Hp: 1,200	*Rpm:* 70 *Psi:* 150
Service:	Cotton spinning. Rope drive.

This was a special design to fit on to the end of the mill, probably replacing a geared drive engine of unknown type, but almost certainly with a vertical shaft. It gave every satisfaction until the mill was closed about 1958. Although widely used for small self-contained engines this design was little used in cotton mills.

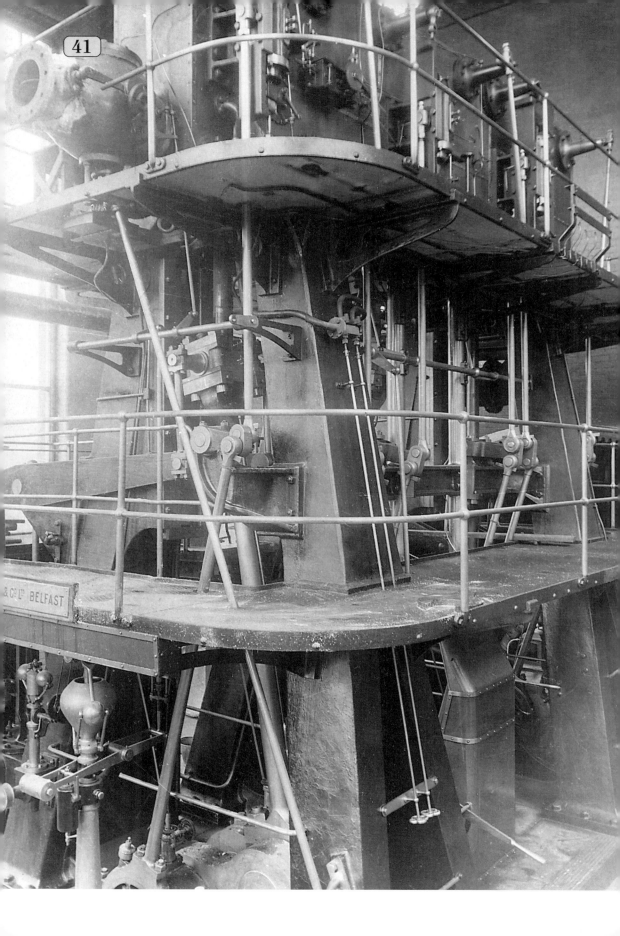

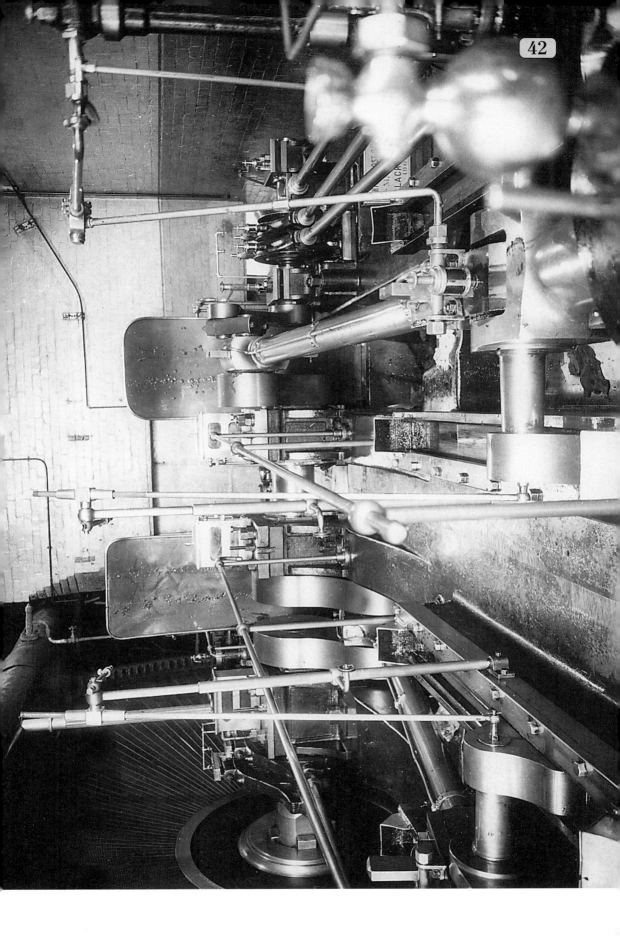

43. Bolton, John Smith & Sons, Bleachers, Great Lever   SER 834

Type: Inverted vertical compound
Photo taken: 1956
Maker and Date: Hick, Hargreaves & Co, Bolton, c. 1905-6
Cylinder/dimensions: 15in and 29.$^1/_2$in x 2ft 0in – Corliss valves
Hp: Approx. 500   *Rpm:* 90   *Psi:* 150
Service: Plant drive. Ropes.

This was run continuously day and night when needed, and was provided with full automatic lubrication for a minimum of supervision. It was Hick, Hargreaves standard design, but with horizontal dash pots for the trip gear. The Corliss valves were all across the crankshaft. There was a heat exchanger in the exhaust pipe partially to heat the process water. The engine was almost unaltered when, after a very busy time, the mill was closed in the early 1960s, and all was scrapped, as the finishing trade fell off.

44. Bolton, The Swan Lane Spinning Co.   SER 633b

Type: Inverted vertical triple expansion condensing
Photo taken: 1954
Maker and Date: George Saxon Ltd., Manchester, No. 493, 1915
Cylinder/dimensions: 27in – 41in – 62in x 4ft 0in – Corliss valves
Hp: 1,800   *Rpm:* 78   *Psi:* 160
Service: Cotton spinning. Rope drive. No. 3 Mill.

No. 3 was tall having nine floors which originally were all driven from the engine. By 1950 the top two floors and later No.6 floor were converted to motor drive for flexibility of production and evening shifts. The 3 Mills were steamed by 10 Lancashire boilers in a single row, which hand fired until 1954, were converted to mechanical stoking. It was as extensive as any spinning mill boiler plant. All of the steam plant was the plain standard designs of the makers, except that Lumb governors were fitted later.

45. Bolton, The Swan Lane Spinning Co.   SER 633a

Type: Two horizontal cross compound
Photo taken: 1954
Maker and Date: George Saxon Ltd., Manchester, 1903 and 1906
Cylinder/dimensions:
Hp: *Rpm:*   *Psi:*
Service: Cotton spinning. Rope drives. No. 1 and 2 Mills.

The mills were in the best tradition of the trade, and all very well kept. The fine column structure between the engines was provided when the mill was built with No.1 only, and the temporary brick wall filling removed when No.2 was finished. The original mule spinning was replaced by electrically driven ring frames in the 1950s, and by 1959, only the preparation load was on the engines. The drives were then re-arranged so that one engine could drive the bottom shafts of the two mills. The mills were set out so accurately originally, that this was readily done by a slight movement of the shafts for the solid couplings.

46. Bolton, Walker & Co., Rose Hill Tannery   SER 1028

Type:	Horizontal single tandem extraction
Photo taken:	1960
Maker and Date:	John Musgrave & Sons (1913) Ltd., Bolton, 1926
Cylinder/dimensions:	27in and 40in x 3ft 0in – Drop valves
Hp: 1,400	*Rpm:* 136 *Psi:* 160
Service:	Electricity heat and power supply to plant.

One of Musgraves last engines, this did them the greatest credit as it ran for 140 hours per week for over 30 years, with little repair', except for the annual overhaul by a first class Musgrave's man as engineer in charge. The alternator was built on to the crankshaft, and was a Mather & Platt 600 kW, No. 20568, with a flange to couple it to the crankshaft and only one (outboard) bearing. Despite its size, there was only a manual ratchet barring attachment, i.e. no barring engine. It passed out anything up to 24,000 lbs of steam at 20 psi to process from the receiver between the high and the uniflow low pressure cylinders, with a compensating governor to maintain constant speed and power conditions. The works were turned over to mains current from the Grid and the engine was removed by 1973.

47. Bolton, Thos. Walmsley & Sons   SER 1120a

Type:	Horizontal non-condensing single cylinder
Photo taken:	1963
Maker and Date:	Unknown, 1870s?
Cylinder/dimensions:	27in x 4ft 0in approx. – Piston valve
Hp: 250	*Rpm:* 30 *Psi:* 70
Service:	Forge rolling mill drive. Direct coupled to roll shaft. Forgemasters.

This was heavily made and well kept, in a house separate from the rolling mill. It had a hand reversing gear with a single eccentric, with gab release to allow hand operation of the steam valve if the rolls jammed, to reverse it to free them. The steam for the works was mainly provided by Rastrick type waste heat boilers on the forge furnaces aided by one on fuel firing. The lagging was particularly good, and the exhaust steam passed through a feed water heater to the atmosphere. It was almost certainly made for driving rolls, and was not an adapted mill engine. The piston was supported by a tail rod and slide.

48. Bolton, Thos. Walmsley & Sons   SER 1120b

Type:	Two inverted vertical single cylinder non-condensing
Photo taken:	1963
Maker and Date:	Hick, Hargreaves & Co., Bolton, 1926
Cylinder/dimensions:	21in x 3ft 0in – Corliss valves
Hp: Approx. 250 each	*Rpm:* 60 *Psi:* 70
Service:	Mill rolls drives. 10 ropes off each flywheel.

Although mounted upon single cast iron bed, these two engines were entirely separate, each driving its own set of rolls, one roughing the forge bar and the other finishing it to size. The drive increase the roll speed to twice that of the engine, and there had been no alterations. This was the last plant in the United Kingdom working the traditional wrought iron, balling up any material that could be obtained, now that making by puddling had ceased. The plant operated upon the traditional method, with the furnace gases passing to Rastrick boilers, some of recent date. There was considerable demand for wrought iron, which has a high resistance to corrosion by air and water, for gates and other exposed structures, and the works will continue as long as supplies can be obtained.

49. Breightmet, nr Bolton, Constantine & Co.   SER 1416b

Type:	Three cylinder with vertical crankshaft
Photo taken:	1970
Maker and Date:	Mather & Platt, Manchester, 1920s
Cylinder/dimensions:	4in x 6in – Slide valves
Hp: 10	*Rpm:* 100 *Psi:* 80
Service:	Tentering machine drive.

Tentering was a finishing process in which cloth was stretched sideways to stabilize it after processing, to eliminate shrinkage and other defects, the machine having pins along the sides which pulled the cloth sideways. The engine was a unique type used only for tentering machines, with a three throw crankshaft driving upwards to a flywheel and pinion, to the large wheel seen at the top. This has four arms each with a hole in it for the tenter rod drive, and each of these is at a different distance from the centre of the shaft so providing four different lengths of travel for the rods carrying the tenter draw pins. The whole was contained in a single massive frame which carried all of the bearings, with one also at the bottom of large gearwheel shaft, the framing being fixed to the floor by four bolts only. Again infinite variation of speed and power were the keynote of the design, and with three cylinders driving at 120 degrees, slow speeds with very heavy pulling power was possible.

50. Breightmet, nr Bolton, Constantine & Co.   SER 1416a

Type:	Double cylinder diagonal
Photo taken:	1970
Maker and Date:	Duncan, Stewart & Co., Glasgow, 1902
Cylinder/dimensions:	$8^{1}/_{2}$ in x 9in – Slide valves
Hp: 20	*Rpm:* 100 *Psi:* 80
Service:	Drying machine drive – direct coupled. Textile finishers.

This shows one of the characteristic finishers' machines with its steam driving engine. The cloth was passed over all the rollers in turn, and these were heated by low pressure steam either from the works mains, or from the engines. The engines were thus self-supporting as the steam had to be supplied in any case, but not all of the finishers used the exhaust steam; in fact, it often was the sign of a finishers, or the rubber trade where these were used, that there might be a dozen exhaust pipes blowing away to waste. Instant and fully variable speed control was essential for finishing and the little engines certainly gave this, but they had almost disappeared by 1970 when this print was taken. There were 17 "tins" or drying drums in this machine, coupled by spur gear wheels, with the cloth passing over all in turn.

51. Briercliffe, Harle Syke, Finsley View Manufacturing Co.   SER 1388

Type:	Horizontal cross compound condensing
Photo taken:	1969
Maker and Date:	Burnley Ironworks Co., 1904
Cylinder/dimensions:	17in and 35in x 4ft 6in – Corliss valves
Hp: 900	*Rpm:* 68 *Psi:* 160
Service:	Weaving shed drive by 18 ropes off 18ft 0in flywheel.

A typical Burnley Ironworks engine of the later period, this drove two weaving sheds by 9 ropes to each shed. It remained as built until the business was closed about 1968, and little repair had ever been required, although with 2,000 looms in the sheds once, it must have been overloaded. The engines were christened *Taylor* and *Emmott* possibly after partners in the concern. Always well kept by responsible owners and engineers, it was in fine condition when, on the closure it was bought by the Science Museum for preservation and is now on display in the East Gallery. The removal cost at least three times the original cost of the engine installed, such has been the increase in prices. It may well be the only engine made by "The Old Shop" to survive.

50

52/53. Briercliffe, Hill End Mill Co.   SER 167 a & b

Type:	Pusher compounded beam
Photo taken:	1935
Maker and Date:	Uncertain (see below)
Cylinder/dimensions:	Beam 28in x 4ft 6in
	Horizontal 16.³/₈in x 4ft 6in
Hp:	*Rpm:* *Psi:*
Service:	Cotton weaving. Spur gear ring, 14ft diameter to 6ft pinion on mainshaft. 13 bevel driven cross loom shafts. Beam 16ft long. Flywheel 16ft diameter.,

The beam engine was said to have been built by Baldwin & Heap of Burnley in 1849, which is doubtful, but the horizontal engine was said to be Robert's make in 1861, and this is possible. It is probable that there had been a smash on the beam since this had a Robert's cylinder with their rocking slide valves, at top and bottom, whilst a new steel connecting rod had also been fitted. An interesting and dangerous feature of the site was that the condensing water lodge was above the engine, so that the condenser discharge had to be pumped away.

54. Briercliffe, Walshaw Mill Co., Harle Syke   SER 1165

Type:	Horizontal single tandem
Photo taken:	1964
Maker and Date:	Pollit and Wigzell, 1905
Cylinder/dimensions:	15in and 26in x 4ft 6in – Corliss valves
Hp: 500	*Rpm:* 70 *Psi:* 180
Service:	Cotton weaving. 20 grooves on 20ft flywheel. Shed designed for 2,000 looms.

Walshaw Mill would have been almost the only four cylinder Pollit & Wigzell made had it been completed, but the left hand side, intended to take the intermediate and other low pressure cylinders was never installed. The plant would certainly have been as heavily loaded as it could be run, for the full 1,000 hp needed for the 2,000 looms intended, but that was usual in the cotton trade where everything was at least 30% overloaded at least once in its lifetime. As it was, this was a highly economical engine, despite the small size of the low pressure cylinder compared with the high steam pressure. An interesting feature was that the high pressure cylinder was placed at the back, whereas Pollit & Wigzells' standard practice was to put the high pressure cylinder nearest to the crank. The mill was weaving cotton with the engine into 1971, but later changes caused the engine to be disused and it was to be removed as the space was needed.

55. Briercliffe, West and Co. Primrose Mill, Harle Syke   SER 1161

Type:	Horizontal single tandem compound
Photo taken:	1964
Maker and Date:	Pollit and Wigzell, 1907
Cylinder/dimensions:	17in and 35in x 4ft 0in – Corliss valves
Hp: 700	*Rpm:* 80 *Psi:* 150 with superheat
Service:	Cotton weaving. 16 rope drive off 20ft flywheel. Shed once contained 1,700 looms.

Again a standard Pollit & Wigzell but with the feature, added later, of increasing the depth of the engine bed near the low pressure cylinder, and providing large circular openings in bosses for the low pressure exhaust valves. It was very heavily loaded for many years, as long as trade was good, although re-spacing later reduced the number of looms. It was one of the last large engines running in the Burnley area and in regular use in 1973 and was of Pollit & Wigzell three piston-rod design. As an example of the complexities of weaving shed construction, this shed contained 22 pairs of bevel wheels for driving the loom cross shafts, and there were 25 bearings on each of the shafts, and a total of 660 bearings on the shafting. Despite this, the engine still drove the whole, since the friction was minimal.

56. Burnley, Wood End Colliery   SER 158a

Type:	Horizontal compound differential
Photo taken:	1935
Maker and Date:	Hathorn, Davey & Co., Sun Foundry, Leeds, c.1890?
Cylinder/dimensions:	24in and 48in x 7ft 0in – Slide valves
Hp: ?	*Rpm:* 4-10 *Psi:* 45
Service:	Mine drainage. 2 ram pumps at pit bottom, driven by two "L" beams, 4 wooden rods also 2 plunger pumps at middle level. Pit shut 1947?

This was the short design, made Pollit-style. The high pressure cylinder was close to the low pressure with twin low pressure piston rods passing beside the high pressure cylinder, with the three rods coupled directly to the crosshead. The differential engine was horizontal, beside the cylinders.

57. Burnley, Wood End Colliery   SER 158b

Type:	Table engines
Photo taken:	1935
Maker and Date:	Unknown
Cylinder/dimensions:	12in x 2ft 0in – Slide valves
Hp:	*Rpm:* *Psi:*
Service:	One used for capstan for pump rods geared to winding barrel. Other used for man riding for shaft inspection. 12ft 0in to top of frame. Flywheel 7ft 0in diameter.

These were unusual in that the whole was contained within the side frame castings; as a rule the table was supported from the bottom bed, but in this, it was supported by the side frames. One of the two table engines was for shaft inspection only, and was less heavily built. Wood End Colliery was the upcast shaft for Bank Hall pit at Burnley, and had a winding engine with 30in cylinders.

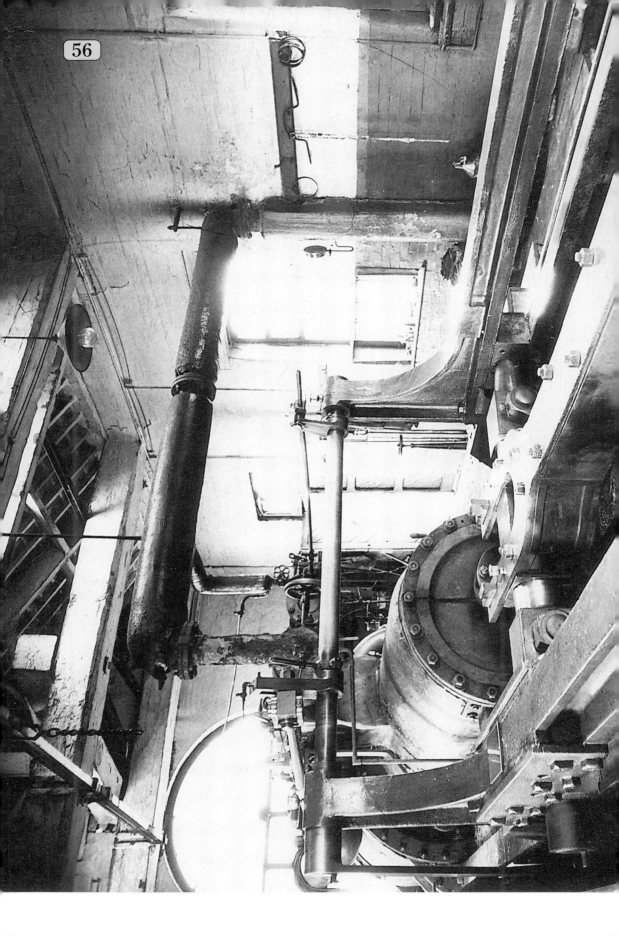

58. Burnley, Bank Hall Colliery   SER 1337b

Type:	Horizontal cross compound non-condensing
Photo taken:	1968
Maker and Date:	Yates & Thom, Blackburn, 1914
Cylinder/dimensions:	Approx. 28in and 56in x 5ft 9in – Drop and Corliss valves
Hp: ?	*Rpm:* 50 *Psi:* 120
Service:	Coal winding. Shafts 500 yards deep. Rope drum 16ft diameter. Tail ropes on cages. No. 4 shaft.

Another of the rare cross compound winding engines, this apparently always exhausted to the atmosphere, as although the colliery was very extensively equipped with brick-works and other plant, there was apparently no low pressure turbine system, although there was electrical generating plant. This was a good example of Yates & Thom's later design, and like the other winder, a Worsley Mesnes piston valve double cylinder, had, despite heavy usage given little trouble. Latterly there were 5 boilers all fired with methane gas for 80 and 120 psi, for the two engines. There were only two cast iron spiders or end supporting plates for this rope drum, and a very unusual feature was that the ropes were wound on in two layers. The entire colliery was closed and all scrapped about 1970.

59. Burnley, The Brennand Mill Co.   SER 974

Type:	Horizontal cross compound
Photo taken:	1959
Maker and Date:	Burnley Ironworks Co., 1899
Cylinder/dimensions:	22in and 44in x 4ft 6in – Corliss valves
Hp: 1,100	*Rpm:* 75 *Psi:* 160
Service:	Cotton weaving. 20 rope drive.

This was probably the largest Burnley Ironworks compound engine in the district, although there were two triple expansion engines as powerful. It was later a room and power mill, but, with over 2,000 looms at one time, it was as large as any in that area. It was the regular Burnley Ironworks Co. design but fitted with tail rods since it was large. Blessed with good engineers, usually of the Capstick family, it was well kept and gave good service. A Lumb regulator gear had been fitted to the original governor, possibly in the 1920s, but little else had been needed. The mill closed with the recession in weaving from cheap Indian imports in the 1960s, and all of the plant was scrapped. It was certainly a credit to the "Old Shop" as the men affectionately termed the Burnley Ironworks, to which they were intensely loyal.

60. Burnley, Burrows & Co., Belle Vue Mill   SER 161

Type:	McNaughted single beam
Photo taken:	1935
Maker and Date:	Wm. Bracewell & Co., Burnley, 1866
Cylinder/dimensions:	$23^1/_2$ in x 2ft 0in and 28in x 4ft 0in – Slide valves
Hp: 150	*Rpm:* $42^1/_2$ *Psi:* 85
Service:	Cotton weaving. Gear drive off flywheel arms, 10ft diameter. Shed mainshaft driven at end, not middle. Beam 13ft 0in long. Closed c. 1960?

This had very little alteration, other than the high pressure cylinder addition, until the mill was closed after 90 years. It would not have closed then, but the boiler was failing, and the cost of a new one was too great. A new flywheel was possibly fitted, but no record remained. The wooden flywheel casing was interesting.

61. Burnley, The Calder Vale Room and Power Co.   SER 705

Type:	Inverted vertical cross compound condensing
Photo taken:	1955
Maker and Date:	Pollit and Wigzell, 1903
Cylinder/dimensions:	16in and 32in x 4ft 0in – Corliss valves
Hp: 400	*Rpm:* 80 *Psi:* 150
Service:	Service for small weavers.

The original shed was small and driven by a double beam engine by a geared flywheel. No history was known, but it is probable that the shed was enlarged when taken over by a concern providing room and power service. Certainly, the Pollit & Wigzell was much more powerful than the beam engine, and at times carried 750 hp on one Lancashire boiler. The original shed drives were not altered, the new section being added apparently as there was only one rope drive pulley. An interesting feature was the horizontal air pump and condenser. All was scrapped in the 1950s when the shed closed.

62. Burnley, Clifton Colliery   SER 170a

Type:	Horizontal double cylinder
Photo taken:	
Maker and Date:	Unknown c. 1890
Cylinder/dimensions:	25ft x 5'0in? – Drop valves
Hp:	*Rpm:* *Psi:*
Service:	Shaft winding. Coal & men. Shaft 260 yds deep.

A neat design with the valves at the corners, and fitted with an ornamental casing over the steam pipe to the valve chests. Four-bar crosshead guides with tail rods on flat slides. Soft packed glands. The winding drum was unusual in that the supporting arms were circular section, and of cast iron (they were usually of tee, or "H" section).

63. Burnley, Clifton Colliery   SER 170b

Type:	Horizontal compound differential tandem
Photo taken:	
Maker and Date:	Hathorn, Davey & Co., Leeds, 1891
Cylinder/dimensions:	27ft & 54ft x 8'0in – Slide valves
Hp:	*Rpm:* *Psi:*
Service:	Main pump, 2-12in rams at pit bottom off "L" bobs. Single lift of 260 yds.

The usual differential design, with massive wooden pitman rods to the pump, with a single lift to surface. The cylinders were not together, and had a single piston rod only to couple the high pressure & low pressure pistons, with twin piston rods to the crosshead. Corliss type restricting valves were fitted in the high pressure cylinder ports, to adjust the speed of the inward and outward strokes, whilst a throttle valve was also fitted between the high pressure & low pressure cylinders. The differential controlling engine was vertical, and at the side.

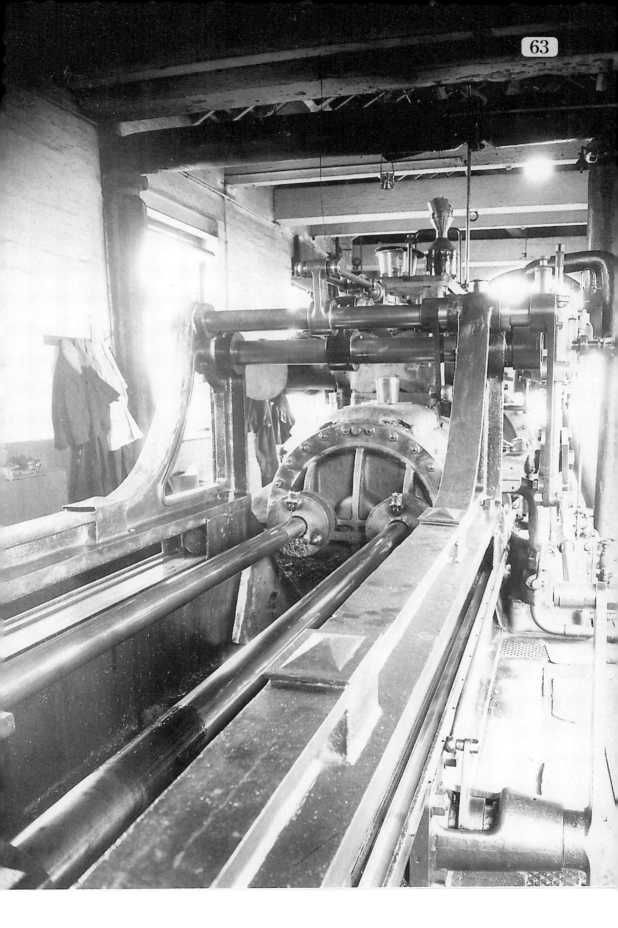

64. Burnley, Clifton Colliery

SER 170c

Type:	Vertical twin cylinder
Photo taken:	
Maker and Date:	unknown
Cylinder/dimensions:	10ft x 2ft 0in – Slide valves
	Flywheel 6ft 0in diameter – 10ft 0in to crankshaft centre
Hp:	*Rpm:* *Psi:*
Service:	Tub haulage on pit bank by moving chains

This was the travelling chain haulage system which was little used in later years outside the Burnley area. The engines were very plain, the frames comprising single castings which were bolted to massive timbers at the top. Several hauling points were driven from a vertical shaft and bevel wheels to drive chain barrels at points up to 60ft 0in away, by shafts below the yard floor, the tubs being traversed by hooking them to the moving chains, by slip hooks. The tubs were traversed around the pit bank to the screens and back to the colliery winding shaft over heavy gradients in this way.

65. Burnley, East Pit

SER 171

Type:	Single cylinder beam engine
Photo taken:	
Maker and Date:	Unknown – date 1839 on house
Cylinder/dimensions:	Dimensions unknown
Hp:	*Rpm:* *Psi:*
Service:	

This was very old and doubtlesss original to the house c. 1839.   The reduction gearing to the pump crankshaft was 3ft 0in & 6ft 0in diameter, the pump crank-shaft 14in square, and the "L" bobs were driven by wooden pitman rods 14in square. It was little used in later years. The pit closed in c. 1938.

66. Burnley, The Ferndale Mill Co.

SER 699

Type:	Horizontal cross compound condensing
Photo taken:	1954
Maker and Date:	Burnley Ironworks Co., 1913
Cylinder/dimensions:	22in and 44in x 5ft 0in – Corliss valves
Hp: 1,000	*Rpm:* 80 *Psi:* 160
Service:	Cotton weaving.

This was almost the last new engine the Burnley Ironworks Co. made, and was large for a weaving shed drive. It needed little repair or other than routine atten-tion in nearly 50 years service until the mills closed about 1960. In later years it was developing about 700 hp on a consumption of some 28 tons of coal per week.

67. Burnley, Sir John Grey, Livingstone Mill   SER 803

Type:	Horizontal cross compound condensing
Photo taken:	1956
Maker and Date:	Wm. Roberts & Sons, Phoenix Foundry, Nelson, 1887
Cylinder/dimensions:	18in and 36in x 5ft 0in – Corliss and slide valves
Hp: 600	*Rpm:* 55 *Psi:* 150
Service:	Cotton weaving. Gear drive.

This was built as a standard Roberts' design, with slide valves on the high pressure cylinder (similar to those on SER 1055, Robert's practice being to fit them on the outer side of the cylinder) and with the valve gear driven from a drag link on the high pressure side crank pin. New boilers and a Corliss valve high pressure cylinder were fitted probably about 1912-14, and as can be seen, the valves had all to be placed at the top of the cylinder, since there was no room in the bed to place the exhaust valves underneath as usual. Otherwise the engine remained as built until with declining trade the mills were to be closed in the early 1960s, and all scrapped. The drive was by a gear ring on the flywheels arms. A new high pressure cylinder was fitted again in 1953.

68. Burnley, The Habergham Room and Power Co.   SER 1125

Type:	Horizontal single tandem
Photo taken:	1963
Maker and Date:	Pollit and Wigzell, 1912
Cylinder/dimensions:	16in and 30in x 3ft 6in – Corliss and slide valves
Hp: 450	*Rpm:* 71 *Psi:* 160
Service:	Room and power supply for small groups of weavers.
	12 rope drive to main shaft off 14ft flywheel.

The mill was designed by Keighley's, architects still in practice in the 1960s, and the engine was named *Susannah Keighley*. The family were probably always closely connected with the business. The engine was a standard Pollit & Wigzell with the piping connections above the bed. Very well kept, it was completely unaltered until the business was closed as the cotton trade fell off in the 1960s. The barring engine was the single cylinder type Pollit & Wigzell used for the smaller engines.

69. Burnley, Haythornthwaite & Sons   SER 1160

Type:	Horizontal cross compound
Photo taken:	1964
Maker and Date:	Burnley Ironworks Co., 1906
Cylinder/dimensions:	16in and 32in x 3ft 6in – Corliss valves
Hp: 450	*Rpm:* 80 *Psi:* 130
Service:	Weaving shed drive by 12 ropes. Grenfell cloth manufacturers.

Another "Old Shop" engine that did extremely well, this ran virtually unaltered, except possibly for a Lumb governor added, until the mill was transferred to the Bishop House Shed, Burnley about 1960. The concern manufactured the very high quality grade Grenfell cloth widely used for Arctic and other severe weather conditions, since nearly impenetrable, it also breathes freely, to release condensation. The plant, engine, boilers and shed was always maintained to high standards. The original two Yates & Thom boilers were replaced by two John Thompson boilers in 1950 were working at 160 psi. The engineer may have been an "Old Shop" man – certainly the engine and plant received every attention. The engine and most of the older looms were scrapped at the change over to Bishop House Shed.

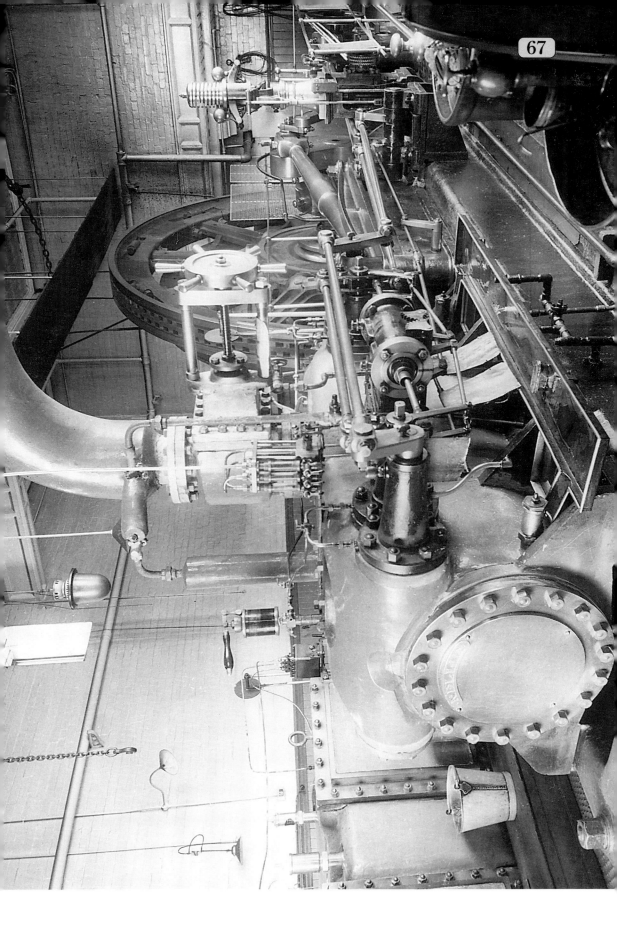

70. Burnley, Healey Wood Mill Co.   SER 168

Type:	McNaught single beam
Maker and Date:	Wm. Bracewell & Co.? 1860
Cylinder/dimensions:	26ft x 2ft 6in 36³/₄ x 5ft 0in – Slide valves
Hp: 350?	*Rpm:* 49 *Psi:* 85 - 100
Service:	Cotton weaving. 3 rope drive to shed, underground shaft and belts to other part.

This was the only engine met fitted with Meyer cut-off valve controlled by a Lumbs governor (Meyer cut-off was usually hand controlled). It was much overloaded, and had been greatly rebuilt. A heavy disc crank had been fitted, together with a massive balance wheel for the rope drive; also at the end of the underground shaft another balance wheel was fitted to assist the momentary overloads in the belt-driven spinning mill. The speed was also increased to gain power, and the installation of electric drive was due to the need for more machines. (electric drives installed 1956).

71. Burnley, Kippax Ltd., Brownside Mill   SER 1101

Type:	Horizontal single tandem
Photo taken:	1962
Maker and Date:	Pollit and Wigzell, 1915
Cylinder/dimensions:	11¹/₂ in and 23in x 2ft 6in – Corliss and slide valves
Hp: 175	*Rpm:* 90 *Psi:* 160
Service:	Cotton weaving. 7 rope drive to shed mainshaft.

The mill was built in the 1850s, and fitted with a beam engine with geared drive, which drove the mill until the Pollit engine was installed. It was a typical Pollit & Wigzell small power engine, and the rather short connecting rod can be seen. It gave virtually no trouble in the fifty years or so that it ran until the drives were changed to electric motors. The mill was kept running during the changeover to the Pollit engine, by installing a separate engine house for the new engine. This was in any case longer than the beam engine, and the rope drive also needed greater length than the original geared drive. The original quotation for the engine alone was £780, with various quotations for the extras, and the final cost, with the alteration to rope drive, i.e. extension of the shaft and rope pulley, was £934. It certainly paid good dividends, far more so than the electric motors, as the plant closed a few years later.

72. Burnley, The Peel Weaving Co., Rose Grove   SER 701

Type:	Horizontal four cylinder triple expansion
Photo taken:	1955
Maker and Date:	Burnley Ironworks Co., Date unknown
Cylinder/dimensions:	17in – 28in – 32in and 32in x 5ft 0in – Corliss valves
Hp: 1,100	*Rpm:* 80 *Psi:* 160
Service:	Cotton weaving.

Burnley Ironworks only made two engines as powerful as this, the other went to Padiham (SER 867), who purchased some spare parts when Peel Mill closed in the 1950s. There were 2,050 looms in the weaving shed, which was considered to be the largest shed in a single block, all driven off one main shaft with 24 bevel wheel drives to the loom shafts. It was always well kept, and needed little attention although frequently fully loaded, but a large output needed high sales rates not easy to maintain during much of the mill's life. All was scrapped on closing.

73. Burnley, Hartley Spencer & Co., Stanley Street   SER 914

Type:	Horizontal single tandem compound
Photo taken:	1958
Maker and Date:	Burnley Ironworks Co., No. 125, 1893
Cylinder/dimensions:	$8^3/_4$ in and $17^3/_4$ in x 2ft 4in – Slide valves
Hp: 90	*Rpm:* 100 *Psi:* 120
Service:	Cotton doubling, and loom heald makers. Scrapped 1960s.

The three-rod tandem design was patented by Pollit & Wigzell in 1872, and they made many hundreds of the type, and a limited number were also made by other engineers after the patent lapsed. The only one known to have been made by the Burnley Ironworks, it was very compact, only requiring a small part of the original beam engine house. It was technically interesting in that the speed was controlled by a shaft governor, operating directly upon the riding cut-off valve of the high pressure cylinder, the low pressure having a plain single slide valve. It drove the floors by ropes from the flywheel which was outside of the engine room, and interesting features were that the main bearing pedestal was cast in one with the engine bed, and the condenser was beside the engine crank, with the air pump driven from the crosshead. It was steamed by a single Cornish boiler made by Anderton of Accrington in 1893, at 120 psi.

74. Burnley, Sutcliffe, Clarkson & Co., Wiseman Street   SER 921

Type:	Horizontal cross compound
Photo taken:	1958
Maker and Date:	Burnley Ironworks Co., c.1880s?
Cylinder/dimensions:	16in and 30 in x 3ft 0in – Corliss and slide valves
Hp: 350	*Rpm:* 60 *Psi:* 140
Service:	Cotton weaving. Gear drive.

This replaced a beam engine which was sited in the large weaving shed, and the horizontal was almost certainly built with slide valve cylinders originally. The Corliss high pressure cylinder was supplied (together with a new boiler by Tinker, Shenton) in 1908, when additions were made to the looms, the sheds now filling almost the entire site. There were considerable increases in the number of looms in the area around that time, and in 1906-7 some 10,000 looms were added in Burnley alone, with similar increases in the whole area up to Skipton. The mahogany lagging was retained on the low pressure cylinder, and other than the substitution of the Corliss cylinder the engine and drives appear to have been little altered. The gear drive was unusual in that the engine ran faster than the second motion shaft, which suggests that the shaft was original for the beam engine, and the faster horizontal engine was coupled in with minimum alteration. It was still in use in 1972.

75. Burnley, W. & T. Thompson, Trafalgar Shed   SER 702

Type:	Horizontal cross compound condensing
Photo taken:	1955
Maker and Date:	Burnley Ironworks Co., 1890
Cylinder/dimensions:	21in and 41in x 3ft 6in – Corliss and slide valves
Hp: 400	*Rpm:* $45^1/_5$ *Psi:* 120
Service:	Cotton weaving. Gear drive. Scrapped 1960.

The engine was installed for O. & J. Folds who then ran the mill, which was carried on by Thompsons until the closure. It was unusual for Burnley Ironworks, having a trunk type frame whereas they later generally used a flat frame with twin slipper guides. It was probably put in when an additional shed was added in 1890, which, as the site was sloping toward the canal, was lower and driven by a short vertical shaft and bevel wheels. Thompsons had also run a spinning mill for their yarn at Rishton, but this closed possibly in the 1920s.

73

76. Burnley, Sharp Thornber, Park Shed   SER 869

Type:	Horizontal cross compound condensing
Photo taken:	1957
Maker and Date:	John Musgrave & Sons, Bolton, 1907
Cylinder/dimensions:	20¹/₂ in and 41in x 4ft 6in – Drop piston valves
Hp: 900	*Rpm:* 80 *Psi:* 150
Service:	Cotton weaving. 22 rope drive. Flywheel 18ft diameter.

This was considered to be the most economical shed engine in Lancashire at the time, and was fitted with Stegen's patent drop piston valves which worked well with high superheat, and which Musgrave adopted in 1905. The economy equalled that of the Grape spinning mill at Royton with the same valves. It was typical of the influence which highly economical Continental designs had upon English practice. The shed mainshaft was driven from one end by a pulley 9ft diameter from the 18ft flywheel, and it once contained 1,764 looms. Latterly, electrical drives were partly installed but the concern closed in the early 1960s, and all was scrapped except possibly a few Northrop looms.

77. Burnley, Waltons, Bishop House Mill, Ryland Street   SER 918

Type:	Horizontal cross compound
Photo taken:	1958
Maker and Date:	Wm. Roberts & Co., Phoenix Foundry, Nelson, 1880s
Cylinder/dimensions:	21in and 40in x 5ft 0in – Slide then Corliss valves
Hp: 800	*Rpm:* 54 *Psi:* 160
Service:	Room and power service to small groups of weavers. Gear drive.

This was a standard Roberts' engine similar to SER 1055 when built, with slide valves but always with gear drive. New Corliss valve cylinders were fitted with new boilers about 1924, the engine ran regularly serving room and power needs until 1952 when, as an inexperienced man was cleaning the engine whilst it was running, his cloth caught in the governor drive ropes, and threw them out of drive. The engine raced away, and before it could be stopped, the flywheel and gear driving ring burst, although happily with limited damage to the engine itself. Various expedients were tried in re-arranging the driving, but none were satisfactory, so in 1954, Wm. Roberts were requested to replace the flywheel and gearing with a set made from the original patterns. This was done and the engine ran for some 8-10 years until the mill was closed owing to poor trade. It was certainly the last geared main drive to be made and, although somewhat noisy, it ran very well. The connecting rod centre boss and four bar guides were typical Roberts of the 1880s.

78. Burnley, Whittlefield Shed   SER 165

Caption on page 124.

78. Burnley, Whittlefield Shed (see page 123)   SER 165

Type:	McNaughted single beam
Photo taken:	1935
Maker and Date:	Wm. Bracewell & Co., Burnley? 1870?
Cylinder/dimensions:	Sizes unknown – slide valves.
Service:	Cotton weaving. Gear drive off flywheel rim to 6ft 0in pinion. Beam 19ft 0in long. Flywheel 20ft 0in diameter.

Built as a single cylinder, this was believed to be McNaughted in the 1880s. The low pressure cylinder was almost certainly the original one, but a new steel connecting rod had been fitted. More power was needed later, so that a diagonal tandem pusher engine was added to the outer end of the crankshaft. This had been removed in the 1930s but the beam engine powered the mill until it closed (possibly about 1947?).

79. Bury, C. W. S, Daisyfield Mill   SER 177a

Type:	Single McNaughted triple expansion beam. (motor ring frames fitted 1963)
Maker and Date:	Buckley & Taylor, Oldham, 1903
Cylinder/dimensions:	28ft x 3ft 0in Corliss Valves (32ft x 4ft 0in) (44ft x 6ft 0in) slide valves
Hp: 1100	*Rpm:* 41 *Psi:* 200
Service:	Cotton Spinning, but had extensive weaving shed as well at one time. 27 ropes to mainshaft. Flywheel diameter 30ft 0in

This replaced an earlier beam engine, possibly when the mill was reorganized in 1903. It was a pure Tattersall late design and was literally unaltered, retaining the Buckley & Taylor brass catch box valve gear, as well as most of the wrought iron parts of the Tattersall specification. The crank boss was notably small on this engine, the boss being 29in, and the shaft 17in diameter; this could have been replaced, but there was no record of this. The two Lancashire boilers were also of Tattersall's design, with the vertical bottom manhole at the front and angle iron furnace rings. Made by Taylor of Marsden, they were works No.1547-8, and were still insured for the original 200 psi pressures at 60 years old.

80. Bury, C.W.S., Daisyfield Mill   SER 177b

Type:	Data as 177a

The machine-finished parallel motion and other parts were typical Tattersall. So too was the beam with the machined levelling pad above the main centre, with similar ones machined upon the end of the beam. The pin centre distances were stamped upon the main parallel motion links; also the gudgeons were drilled for oiling as well as having oil holes in each brass. There was no engine room crane, but massive girders were built into the engine room roof, for lifting heavy parts.

81. Bury, C.W.S., Daisyfield Mill   SER 177c

Type:	Data as 177a

The new engine house was built out from the mill, and the bearing pads for the beam cross girder can be seen built into the wall. The weaving shed was at the left and was driven by ropes back from the second motion by the shaft and coupling seen projecting, to bevel wheels and a shaft along the side of the shed.

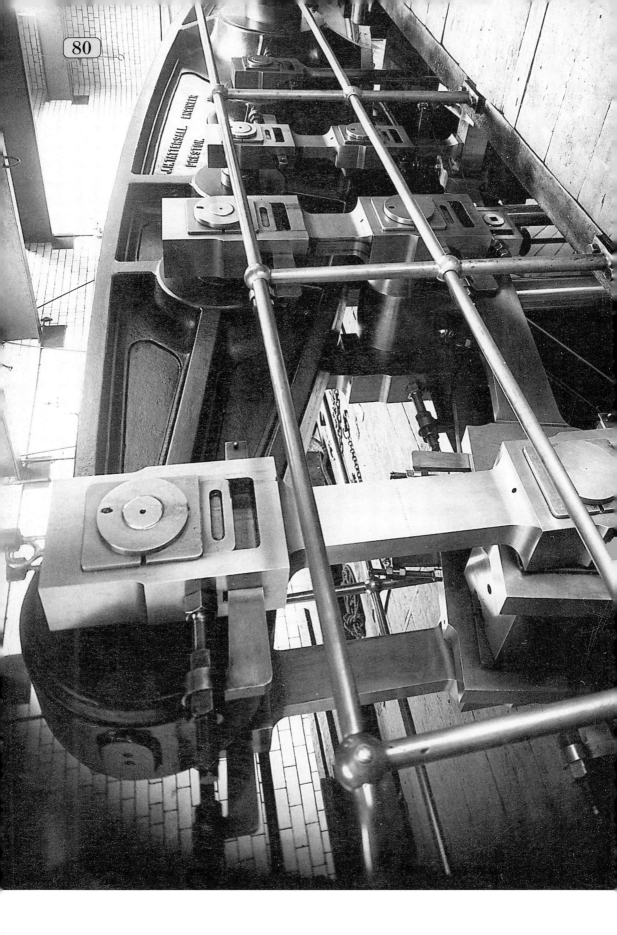

82. Bury, Entwistle & Co.   SER 1123

Type:	Horizontal single tandem
Photo taken:	1963
Maker and Date:	S. S. Stott & Co., Haslingden, 1911
Cylinder/dimensions:	Approx. 12in and 24in x 3ft 0in – Corliss and slide valves
Hp: 300	*Rpm:* 75 *Psi:* 140
Service:	Textile Mills. No. 1 engine. Cotton spinning and weaving. 12 rope drive off 12ft flywheel.

There had been beam engines at the mills once, replaced by tandem horizontals, and later by Stott tandems, possibly. One Stott engine was replaced by motor drives in 1962, No. 1 continuing at work certainly until the late 1960s. It latterly drove the No.s 1 and 2 weaving sheds, almost entirely with rope drives even for the loom shafts, a number of the pulleys being on the outside of the shed. There were at least 11 shafts thus rope driven, some in a shed 12 ft below the engine level. The engine was typical Stott design; very stiff and solid. The condenser was Benn's patent type, rope driven from the engine crankshaft and was very quiet. The rope drive was very quiet, also; there were several multiple pulleys for the shed drives.

83. Bury, The Lancashire Cotton Corp.   SER 1009

Type:	Horizontal four cylinder triple expansion
Photo taken:	1959
Maker and Date:	J. & E. Wood, Bolton, 1906
Cylinder/dimensions:	$23\frac{1}{2}$in – $33\frac{1}{2}$in – 41in x 5ft 0in – Corliss valves
Hp: 2,000	*Rpm:* 68 *Psi:* 200
Service:	Cotton spinning. 46 ropes off 26ft flywheel.

Similar to Coppull, this again was standard J & E Wood's design, and it is probable that the mills were designed by the same architect, but Pilot had no side engine room windows. It was, however, very low relative to the mill, and was probably the only large Lancashire spinning mill engine which was not entered by steps, as it was on the mill yard level, and with the boilers completely below the yard level. The boilers were usually lower than the yard for easy coal delivery, but at Pilot the boiler tops were entirely below the yard. This again had more than the usual ropes for the power, and had a Lumb governor fitted in later years. Very well kept, the plant was later scrapped when the mill was closed.

84. Bury, Peel Mills   SER 632 (1)

Type:	Horizontal cross compound
Photo taken:	1954
Maker and Date:	John Musgrave & Sons, Bolton, 1886
Cylinder/dimensions:	32in and 56in x 9ft 0in – Corliss and slide valves
Hp: 1,400	*Rpm:* 52 *Psi:* 120
Service:	Cotton spinning. No. 1 Mill.

This was Musgrave's standard engine of the period, entirely as built even to the governor.

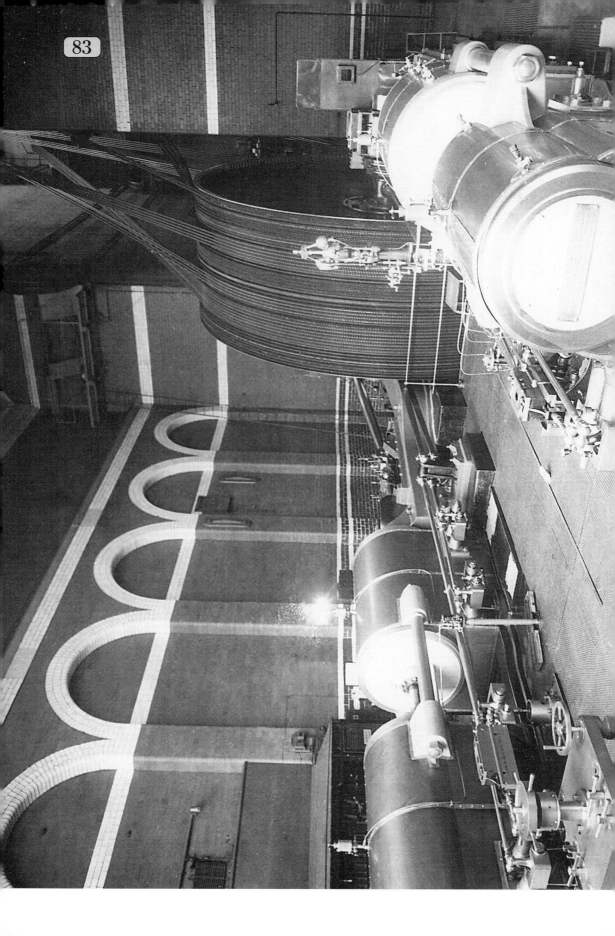

83

85. Bury, Peel Mill   SER 632 (2)

Type:	Non dead centre vertical quadruple expansion
Photo taken:	1954
Maker and Date:	John Musgrave & Sons, Bolton, 1892
Cylinder/dimensions:	18in –26in – 37in – 54in x 4ft 6in – Corliss valves
Hp: 1,600	*Rpm:* 75 *Psi:* 160
Service:	Cotton spinning. No. 2 Mill.

The maker's plate stated that this was made to Fleming and Ferguson's patent and it gave very good service overloaded for over 60 years, when electrical drives were installed. It was a standard example of which Musgrave made over 50 in about 15 years to 1908, but all steam plant was scrapped later, the mills running into the late 1960s. It was the first which Musgrave made to this design.

86. Calder Vale, nr. Garstang, The Barnacre Weaving Co.   SER 904

Type:	Horizontal single tandem
Photo taken:	1958
Maker and Date:	Possibly W. & J. Yates, Blackburn, 1870?
Cylinder/dimensions:	15in and 27in x 3ft 6in – Slide valves
Hp: 160	*Rpm:* 60 *Psi:* 70
Service:	Cotton weaving. Rope drive.

This may have been built as a single cylinder engine with the condenser behind the cylinder, and later changed to tandem compound by placing a low pressure cylinder where the condenser was originally. A Lumb governor was fitted, possibly in the 1920s. There was water power on the site, originally a water wheel and later a turbine, but this was disused as the water flow dropped. The engine ran in reverse, although latterly driving by rope it was almost certainly a gear drive originally. The concern was started in 1845 and ran with reasonable success until it was closed about 1958, when all was scrapped.

87. Chadderton, Ace Spinning Mill   SER 730

Type:	Horizontal cross compound condensing
Photo taken:	1955
Maker and Date:	Urmson & Thompson, Hathershaw Ironworks, Oldham, 1914
Cylinder/dimensions:	31in and 62in x 5ft 0in
Hp: 2,400	*Rpm:* 63 *Psi:* 180
Service:	Cotton Spinning. 48 rope drive. Spinning started 1921.

The mill was due for completion in 1914, and the engines and the four boilers were in store on the site for most of the War period. It was a very good engine and mill, possibly as successful as any of the later ones. It was a standard Urmson & Thompson engine although they did not make many, and were largely mill gearing and repair specialists. The high centre line again was noticeable. The general finish was very high, and maintenance good. The mill was later converted to electrically driven ring spinning frames, and the engine scrapped.

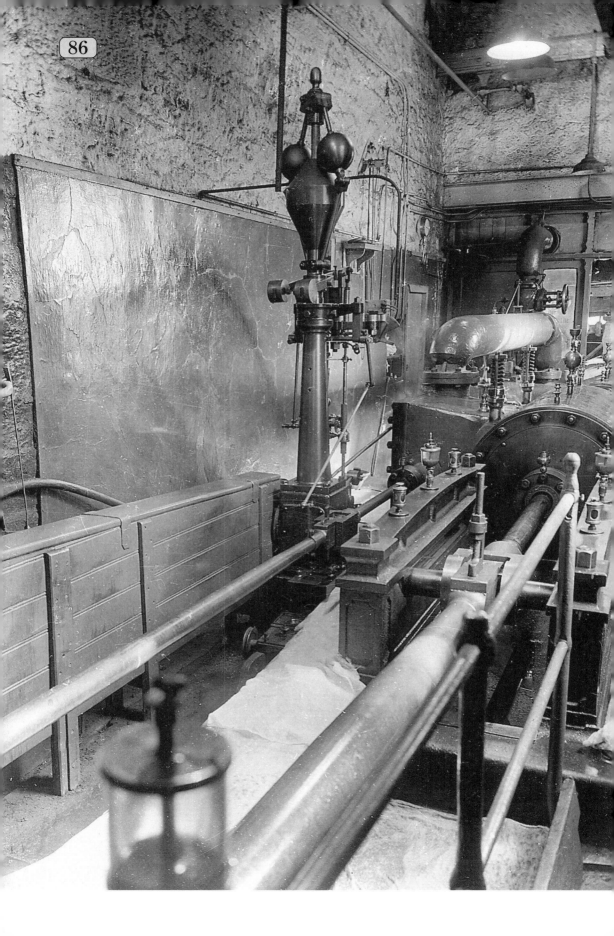

88. Chadderton, Glenby Mill   SER 498

Type:	Horizontal twin tandem compound condensing
Photo taken:	1952
Maker and Date:	Buckley & Taylor, Oldham, Date unknown
Cylinder/dimensions:	22in and 45in x 6ft 0in – Corliss H.P. and slide L.P. valves
Hp: 1,500	*Rpm:* 44 *Psi:* 160
Service:	Cotton spinning. Coarse count. Geared drive.

This was built as the standard Buckley & Taylor slide, valve twin tandem, and new Corliss valve high pressure cylinders were fitted by Scott and Hodgson in 1908, plus new high pressure boilers. Otherwise the engine was unaltered, except for a new flywheel which was fitted in 1930. The mill probably closed in the spindles redundancy scheme, 1960.

89. Chadderton, Gorse Mill   SER 603

Type:	Horizontal cross compound condensing
Photo taken:	1953
Maker and Date:	Urmson & Thompson, Oldham, 1906
Cylinder/dimensions:	26in and 56in x 5ft 0in – Corliss valves
Hp: 1,600	*Rpm:* 65 *Psi:* 180
Service:	Cotton spinning.

Named *Sarah* and *Hannah* this shows the very high engine centre line of some of Urmson & Thompson's half dozen engines, all built for spinning mills. They were similar in design, with Corliss trip gear resembling Buckley & Taylor's brass catch box type. It ran the mill with little trouble until it closed in about 1960.

90. Chadderton, Junction Mill, Middleton Junction   SER 793

No data available.

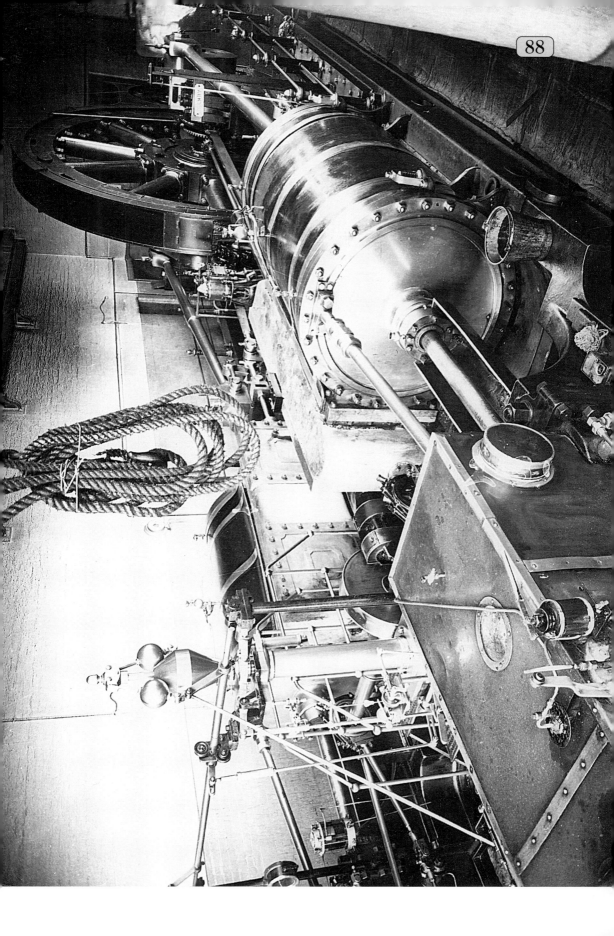

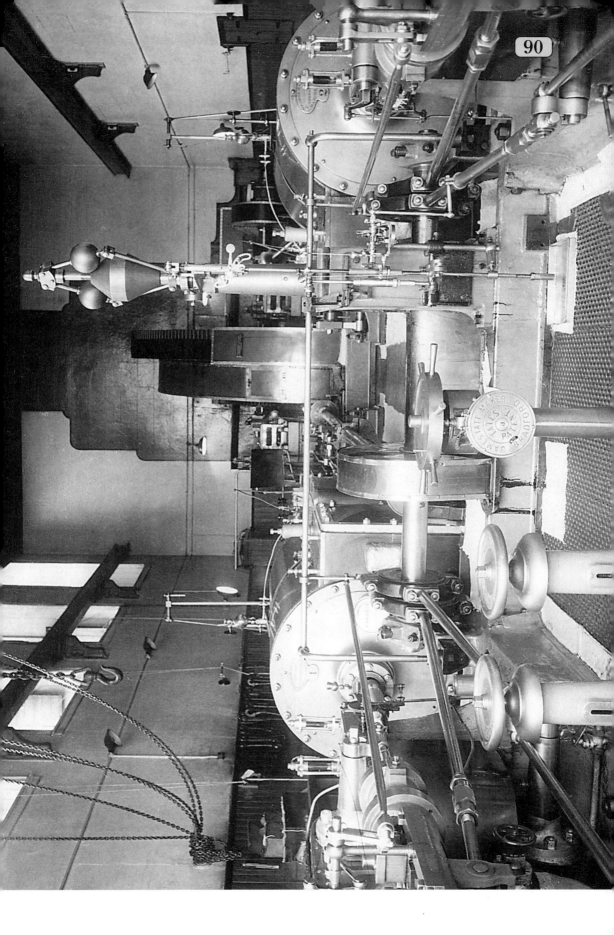

91. *Chadderton, The Sun Mill Co.*   SER 755

Type:	Inverted vertical triple expansion
Photo taken:	1955
Maker and Date:	Scott & Hodgson, Guide Bridge, 1902
Cylinder/dimensions:	29in – 45in and 73in x 4ft 6in – Corliss valves
Hp: 3,500	*Rpm:* 75 *Psi:* 220
Service:	Cotton spinning. 54 ropes. Flywheel 22ft 0in diameter.

This was the largest vertical-engine in the United Kingdom and the low pressure cylinder was, at 73in bore, the largest in Lancashire mills; it is possible that it was the largest ever fitted in a spinning mill. The mill was heavily loaded and a new high pressure cylinder some 3 inches larger than the original was fitted in the early 1950s, and the engine (as indeed most of Scott & Hodgson's) gave little trouble despite heavy oversize loads. The mill was closed and everything scrapped in the cotton trade re-organisation scheme in 1960. Sun Mill when founded in 1860, was the first of the joint stock cotton mills, in which public investment was invited. The original engines were probably horizontal twin with geared drive.

92. *Chorley, James Fletcher & Co., Brook Street Mill*   SER 780

Type:	McNaughted single beam
Photo taken:	1955
Maker and Date:	John Musgrave & Sons, Bolton, 1850 and 1880
Cylinder/dimensions:	26in x 4ft 0in and 20in x 2ft 0in – Drop and slide valves
Hp: Approx. 200	*Rpm:* 35 *Psi:* 100
Service:	Weaving shed. 196 looms. Geared drive.

Built as a single cylinder engine in 1850, it ran thus until new boilers were needed in 1880 as well as more power and it was then McNaught compounded. There was no record of a breakdown, but the low pressure cylinder, connecting rod, and possibly the beam all appeared to have been renewed. The low pressure was always slide valve, and the high pressure cylinder had Musgrave's drop valves and cut-off under governor control. The business was retained in the cotton trade re-organisation scheme of 1960, but regrettably was compelled to close from bad trade in 1963, when all was scrapped.

93. *Chorley, J. H. Gillett & Sons, Crosse Hall Mills*   SER 610

Type:	Inverted vertical grid valve cross compound
Photo taken:	1953
Maker and Date:	Ferranti Ltd., 1898
Cylinder/dimensions:	13in and 28in x 1ft 1in – Two grid valves.
Hp: 350	*Rpm:* 120 *Psi:* 120
Service:	Weaving shed drive. Ropes and gears.

This was one of two similar engines supplied to Lambeth electricity supply system in 1898 (Ferranti's order No.581) each fitted with a 250 kW generator upon the crank-shaft, at a total cost of £3,596. Load growth was evidently great, as they were disposed of less than two years later, and Gillett's purchased this one in about 1900. It ran the weaving shed with 850 looms for over 60 years, and was purchased back by Ferranti Ltd for preservation as the last remaining example of their engines, and is now preserved in very good conditions at Hollinwood. In this type there are only two valves, whereas the larger Ferranti designs had four plain grid valves.

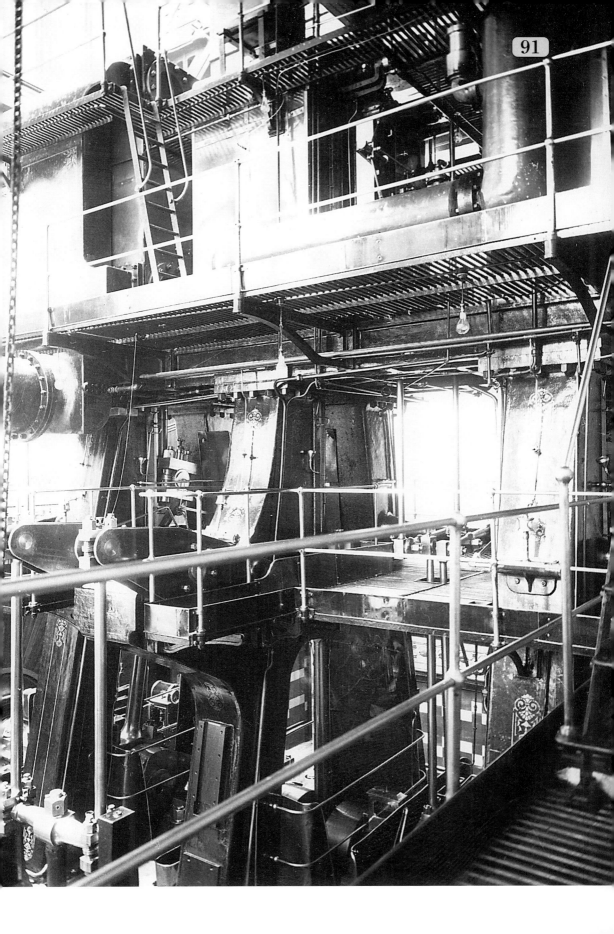

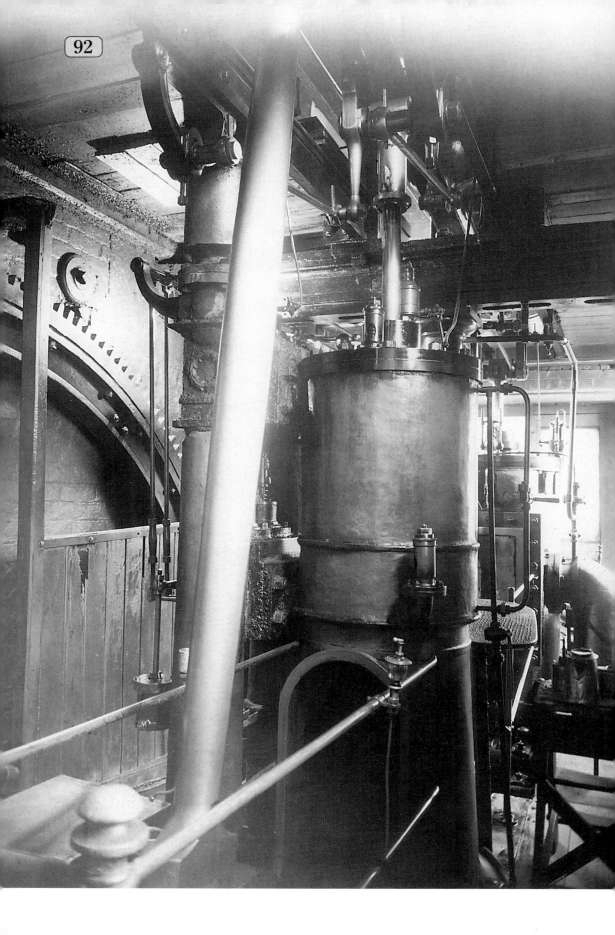

94. Chorley, J. H. Gillett & Sons, Crosse Hall Mills   SER 611

Type:	Double "A" frame cross compound beam
Photo taken:	1953
Maker and Date:	Clayton, Goodfellow, Blackburn, 1856
Cylinder/dimensions:	21in and 36½in x 4ft 0in – Corliss and slide valves
Hp:	*Rpm:* *Psi:*
Service:	Derelict spinning mill engine.

This had driven the spinning mill until it was destroyed by fire some years before and the whole lay derelict, until the site was cleared when Gillett's closed. Built as a double-cylinder slide valve with cylinders of about 36in bore, it was converted to compound by Musgrave of Bolton by fitting Corliss valve high pressure and slide valve low pressure cylinders in 1893-4. Boilers for higher steam pressure were installed but no other alterations were made in the engine which then ran economically for many years.

95. Chorley, Wm. Lawrence & Co. Ltd.   SER 984

Type:	Horizontal cross compound
Photo taken:	1959
Maker and Date:	Unknown, 1887?
Cylinder/dimensions:	15in and 24in x 3ft 6in – Slide valves
Hp: Approx. 250	*Rpm:* 50 *Psi:* Approx. 120
Service:	Textile mills. Cotton spinning and weaving. Gear drive to weaving shed and a four-floor mill.

There were three engines on the site, but all were stopped and electric driving was in use by 1959. This engine drove one section, with a tandem, and vertical triple expansion engines for the rest. There was no nameplate on this, and the maker was not known, but it was said to have driven electrical generating plant at a Manchester exhibition in c. 1887. Since Mather & Platt were prominent in this business then, it is probably of their make, and was very plain, with throttle governing, plain slide valves without cut-off gear, and with single slipper guides for the crossheads. The drive was by gear teeth sectors on the flywheel arms and the only addition had been a Lumb governor possibly in the early 1920s. All of the steam plant was scrapped in the 1960s.

96. Chorley, The Talbot Spinning and Weaving Co.   SER 802

Type:	Two horizontal twin tandem triple expansion
Photo taken:	1956
Maker and Date:	J. & E. Wood, Bolton, 1907
Cylinder/dimensions:	Mill engine – 24in – 36-40in and 40in x 5ft 0in – 1,800hp.
	Shed engine – 16in – 26in – 30in and 30in x 4ft 6in – 700hp.
Hp: 2,500	*Rpm:* 60 *Psi:* 200
Service:	Cotton spinning and weaving.

Talbot was a splendid mill which was always successful, and the power plant was as fine as the buildings. The engines were typical J. & E. Wood design, with the valves below, and until a mass of switchgear spoiled the view when fitted to the columns between the two engines, it must have been a fine sight, as the illustration copied from J & E Woods catalogue of c. 1909 shows. The engines remained as built until, with the conversion to electric driving, all the steam plant, including the seven boilers still carrying the original 200 psi were scrapped. Two Cochran Chieftain boilers were then installed for the heating load. The round upper engine room windows were often met in that area.

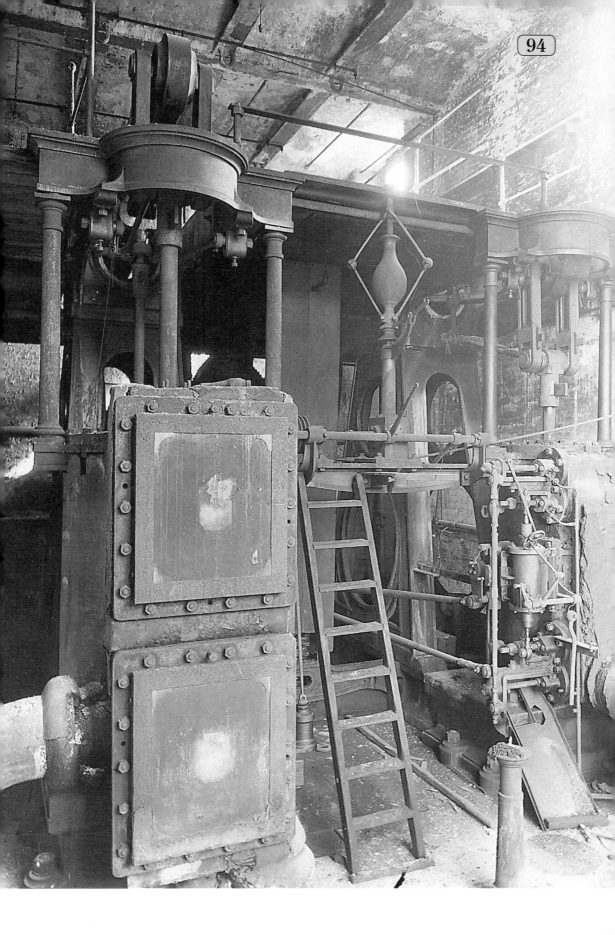

97. Chorley, W. and C. Widdows, Canal Mill SER 824

Type:	Horizontal side by side compound
Photo taken:	1956
Maker and Date:	Wood Bros., Sowerby Bridge, 1895
Cylinder/dimensions:	19in and 36in x 3ft 0in – Corliss valves
Hp: 600	*Rpm:* 90 *Psi:* 150
Service:	Cotton spinning. Rope drive to original gearing.

Canal Mill was built in 1855 with a beam engine probably by Knight & Wood of Bolton with a vertical shaft to the five mill floors. The beam engine was McNaught compounded by Musgrave, (cylinder 40in x 5ft 6in) in 1876 and the gearing and vertical shaft (which was supported upon a bracket upon the wall of the mill) was retained until the mill closed about 1958. Oil at 1,000 psi was pumped in to keep the foot-step cool. The horizontal engine was fitted with Dobson's Corliss trip gear, and probably replaced the Wood trip gear, as it is unlikely that Wood Bros., supplied any but their type, and a change from that was very rare. Possibly done by G.Saxon?

98. Church, W. F. Chambers & Co., Primrose Mill SER 1145

Type:	Horizontal cross compound
Photo taken:	1964
Maker and Date:	Ashton, Frost & Co., Blackburn, 1884?
Cylinder/dimensions:	$17\frac{1}{2}$in and $36\frac{1}{2}$in x 4ft 6in – Corliss and slide valves
Hp: 350	*Rpm:* 42 *Psi:* 150
Service:	Cotton weaving. Geared drive to shed main shaft.

The horizontal engine replaced a beam engine in 1884, and was almost certainly built with a slide valve high pressure cylinder. This was replaced by the Corliss valve-cylinder in 1908, when the present boiler was supplied. The horizontal engine may not have been made by Ashton, Frost & Co, but the later high pressure cylinder certainly was. Some detail features resembled Roberts earlier engines, and their works were not far away, at Nelson. The only change in the engine seems to have been the high pressure cylinder, and governor. The engine was developing 250 h.p. in 1963, when the plant was taken over on Chamber's move from Accrington: there was every intention of continuing to keep running with the engine, and it was so for some five years at least.

99. Clitheroe, James Thornber, Holmes Mill SER 1193

Type:	Horizontal cross compound
Photo taken:	1965
Maker and Date:	Clayton, Goodfellow, Blackburn, No. 544 and 5, 1910
Cylinder/dimensions:	15in and 30in x 2ft 6in – Corliss and slide valves
Hp: 350	*Rpm:* 66 *Psi:* 100
Service:	Cotton weaving. 9 rope drive from 12ft flywheel.

The plant was driven by a beam engine, which had been altered by Saxon to give more power, but with increasing load, a new engine was needed by 1910. This was a typical Clayton, Goodfellow weaving shed engine which ran unaltered into the 1970s, driving on to the original shed mainshaft, with ropes replacing the gears of the beam engine. The business was old-established and likely to continue as long as trade allowed.

100. Colne, Thos. Mason, Primet Mills   SER 506b

Type:	Horizontal cross compound condensing
Photo taken:	
Maker and Date:	Wm. Roberts & Sons., Phoenix Foundry, Nelson, 1896
Cylinder/dimensions:	16ft & 30ft x 4ft 0in – Slide valves
Hp: 250	*Rpm:* 90 *Psi:* 90
Service:	Weaving shed drive.

The No. 2 shed, completed in a great expansion period, illustrates the changes that had taken place in engine design over some 40 years. It was still a sound basic design, plain, solid and reasonably economical which could be relied upon to keep running regularly with little attention. The open flywheel arms although losing power, by windage were a saving in cost and left the flywheel structure readily visible. The high pressure cylinder in the left foreground shows the unusual Roberts feature of the high pressure slide valves being on the outer side of the cylinder (they were usually placed between the cylinders) and also, the Roberts cross grid cut off valves. The No. 2 shed was replaced by the increased capacity of No. 1, when it was re–equipped with automatic looms in the early 1960s.

101. Colne, Pickles & Co., Bankfield Mill   SER 1100

Type:	Horizontal single tandem
Photo taken:	1962
Maker and Date:	Wm. Roberts & Sons., Phoenix Foundry, Nelson, 1927
Cylinder/dimensions:	Approx. 12in and 21in x 3ft 0in – Corliss valves
Hp: 300	*Rpm:* 90 *Psi:* 130
Service:	Cotton weaving. 7 rope drive to sheds. 303 looms in 1956.

This was almost certainly the last new engine both to go into a Colne weaving shed, and to be made by Roberts. It was their late design with Whitehead trip gear for the Corliss valves, and replaced the original engine when more power was required for the new shed added at the time. There was probably never a beam engine there, but the earlier horizontal engine drove to the first shed by a leather belt some 36in wide. The boiler was dated 1903, and may have been for the first engine, and ran the plant until electrical drives were installed, when the engine was scrapped.

102. Colne, E. & P. Riley, Walk Mill   SER 1126

Type:	Horizontal cross compound and tandem
Photo taken:	1963
Maker and Date:	Wm. Roberts & Sons., Phoenix Foundry, Nelson, 1907-8
Cylinder/dimensions:	18in and 30in x 3ft 6in (cross compound)
	13$\frac{1}{2}$in and 26in x 3ft 0in (tandem)
Hp: 600-350	*Rpm:* 75 *Psi:* 160
Service:	Cotton weaving. Two sheds with separate engines. 8 and 10 rope drives.

This was an old established business and was driven by a large beam engine, until the re-organization of 1908. The two sheds were quite independent, and latterly the larger engine only was sufficient to maintain the production in the 1960s. There were two boilers by Yates & Thom, new with the engines, retaining the original working pressure when 60 years old. The business probably closed in 1970, and the plant was almost certainly all scrapped.

103. Colne, Andrew Swire, Railway Street Mills   SER 507

Type:	Horizontal single crank tandem triple expansion
Photo taken:	1952
Maker and Date:	W. & J. Yates, Blackburn? 1890
Cylinder/dimensions:	9$^1/_4$in – 14$^1/_4$in and 23in bores x 3ft 6in stroke
Hp: 110	*Rpm:* 79 *Psi:* 110
Service:	Cotton weaving shed drive.

This was designed to develop 250 hp, and possibly purchased from an exhibition, when the mill was rebuilt upon a very old mill site. The engine drove directly onto the shed mainshaft, and since this was near to the side wall of the shed, the flywheel was partly outside within a sheet metal casing. The mill was said to have been in the silk trade once, but was finally closed in 1956, and the chimney had been removed by 1962, when the premises were unused.

104. Colne, The Vivary Bridge Estates Co.   SER 884

Type:	Horizontal single tandem condensing
Photo taken:	1957
Maker and Date:	Wm. Sharples, Ramsbottom, Date unknown
Cylinder/dimensions:	Approx. 16in and 30in x 3ft 0in – Corliss and slide valves
Hp: 250	*Rpm:* 84 *Psi:* 100
Service:	Room and power supply. 10 rope drive.

Sharples did not construct many larger mill type engines, mainly making looms and finishing machinery. The four-bar crosshead guides and the marine type connecting rod ends were unusual features in mill engines, and this remained largely unaltered, and had required little attention until the plant was closed and all scrapped about 1960. A Lumb governor had been fitted, probably in the 1920s. This engine retained the Sharples Corliss trip gear, which was similar to Musgrave's later type. Generally it was a good plain mill engine with few unusual details.

105. Coppull, Coppull Ring Mill   SER 1008

Type:	Horizontal four cylinder triple expansion
Photo taken:	1959
Maker and Date:	J. & E. Wood, Bolton, 1906
Cylinder/dimensions:	19$^1/_2$in – 31in – 34in and 34in x 4ft 0in – Corliss valves
Hp: 1,250	*Rpm:* 68 *Psi:* 200
Service:	Cotton spinning. Ring frames. 36 rope drive from 26ft flywheel.

Coppull was a well-planned mill with money laid out for an adequate plant at the start, and it paid well in its 60 years as a steam mill. This was a typical J & E Wood engine, in very good condition and very well kept until it was scrapped in 1966 on conversion to motor drives. The engine room windows were not large, yet the engine room was attractive for its roomy layout. The engine was rather high over the mill yard with much of the drive below the engine, on the lower floors. The Mavis Mill was similar and on the same site; although a different concern, it had shared the same chimney and cooling water lodge. The arrangement was said to have worked indifferently when there were heavy demands for steam and water, but Mavis was far less successful than Coppull. A Lumb governor was added later.

103

106. Darwen, Darwen Hope Co., Bank Top Mill   SER 829

Type:	Horizontal cross compound
Photo taken:	1956
Maker and Date:	J. & R. Shorrock and Co., Darwen, 1889
Cylinder/dimensions:	18in and 32in x 3ft 6in – Corliss and slide valves
Hp: 300	*Rpm:* 62 *Psi:* 120
Service:	Cotton weaving. Gear drive.

The history of the mill and engine were uncertain, but it was believed to have had a beam engine previously. It was very rare to find a Shorrock engine as, although they did make some engines, the main business was as a foundry making looms and finishing machinery. It was the only Shorrock engine known in 1956 and was very rare as a drive since the shed mainshaft was divided in two at the engine, with the flywheel well out into the shed, and the halves of the mainshaft each driven by a separate pinion. A new boiler was supplied by Yates & Thom in 1916, with a superheater, but by 1953 with reduced load, the steam pressure was lowered to 50 psi. A new steel driving pinion was fitted to the right hand side in 1953, but all was closed and scrapped in 1960.

107. Darwen, Mr Grimes, Sunnybank Paper Mill   SER 1404

Type:	Vertical single cylinder non-condensing
Photo taken:	1970
Maker and Date:	Possibly Rushton's Foundry, Darwen, 1850s?
Cylinder/dimensions:	$10^{1}/_{2}$ in x 2ft 0in – Slide valve
Hp: 10	*Rpm:* 70 *Psi:* 60
Service:	Drove glue coating machines for linen backing.

This was an old cotton mill latterly taken by Mr Grimes's family for making the heavy glazed-face paper glued to linen backing for folding maps. The old boiler was condemned and cut up for scrap, and latterly steam was purchased from a nearby mill and exhausted to the atmosphere. The mill had three floors and there was no evidence that it had driven by gearing at any time, and probably, as latterly, had driven by belt to the upper floors as well when in cotton trade. All of the paper machinery was on the ground floor and driven from the single mainshaft, again by belts. The original boiler was close to the engine, and probably Cornish, about 5ft x 24ft long. The date was difficult even to guess, as the flywheel was certainly a very old design, and the engine very light. When the little mill closed about 1971, the local authority responsibly took the engine into its charge, and it may well later be exhibited, either as SER 1405, in the open, or in a museum.

108. Open space in Darwen   SER 1405

Type:	Horizontal cross compound condensing
Photo taken:	1970
Maker and Date:	J. & E. Wood, Bolton, Early 1900s
Cylinder/dimensions:	Approx. 16in and 30in x 3ft 6in – Corliss valve
Hp: Approx. 350	*Rpm:* 80 *Psi:* 160
Service:	Exhibited in open.

There were two J. & E. Wood engines in the Bowling Green Mill, Darwen, each driving a weaving shed. The two engines were in one room, and this is almost certainly one of them, and also the last J.& E. Wood engine (except Trencherfield) to remain in Lancashire, but one remains in Yorkshire (at Beaumont's, Huddersfield). The removal of the Darwen engine was well done, and the open site emphasises the very neat lines of the design. It had not been altered in any way during some 60 years of service, so remains a typical example of J & E Wood's work; neat and attractive. The Corliss valves all below the cylinder, and with the steam stop valve near to the high pressure cylinder valve gear, are features which they adopted over many years.

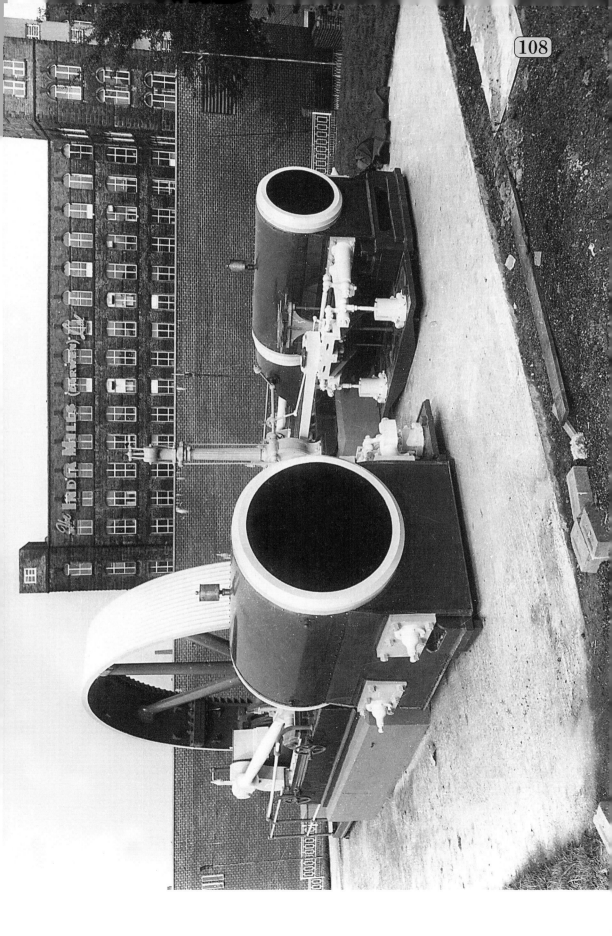

109. Darwen, The Provident Mill Co., Prospect Mill   SER 1096

Type:	Horizontal cross compound
Photo taken:	1962
Maker and Date:	Ashton, Frost & Co., Blackburn, 1906
Cylinder/dimensions:	17in and 30in x 4ft 0in – Corliss and slide valves
Hp: 350	*Rpm:* 40 *Psi:* 150
Service:	Cotton weaving. Drive by 14 cotton ropes, to shed main shaft.

This almost certainly replaced a gear driving, possibly a beam engine, but it did not run in reverse as was usual with such a change of drive. It was certainly an old engine room, and the drives to the looms may have been altered to suit the reversed engine direction. It was a typical Blackburn shed engine, plain and economical, and had the usual feed pump drive from the low pressure valve spindle tail rod, which can be seen in the lower right-hand corner of the plant. The engine could have been made by Yates & Thom of Blackburn, and only the cylinders were by Ashton, Frost & Co., but there was little positive record of the plant. All was scrapped in the cotton trade re-organisations of the 1960s.

110. Droylsden, The Lancashire Cotton Corporation, Saxon Mill
SER 1095

Type:	Horizontal cross compound
Photo taken:	1962
Maker and Date:	D. Adamson & Co., Dukinfield, 1907
Cylinder/dimensions:	$27^1/_2$in and 56in x 5ft 0in – Wheelock, then Corliss valves.
Hp: 1,600	*Rpm:* 65 *Psi:* 160
Service:	Spinning mill. Drive by 36 ropes.

This was one of the few Wheelock valve engines fitted into Lancashire cotton spinning mills, but the original cylinders were replaced in 1944 by the very fine Saxon Corliss valve cylinders seen in the print. These were designed to use super-heated steam and were quite economical. The rope drives were to the three upper spinning, and the lower preparation floors of the mill, but the mill was gradually changed over to motor-driven ring spinning frames and by 1963 less than half of the original mule spinning frames remained. With the full installation of ring frames the engine was scrapped by 1967 and the mill kept running.

111. Daisy Nook, Failsworth, The Ashton Canal   SER 503

Type:	Direct acting beam pump
Photo taken:	1952
Maker and Date:	Unknown, early 1800s?
Cylinder/dimensions:	36in x 7ft 6in – Drop valves
Hp:	*Rpm:* *Psi:*
Service:	Lifting water to top lock pound.

This may have come from a colliery, but it was certainly a very early design, with steam valves for the lower end, and the steam continuously acting upon the top of the piston, i.e. Watt's design of the 1780s, not the later Cornish cycle. The pump rod capstan seen in the front was always man-operated. The pump rod was of cruciform section cast iron, which, with the parallel motion at the pump end, were all very early features. After many years of disuse it became unsafe through vandalism, and was dismantled, which was regrettable being a very rare type.

112. Failsworth, Regent Mill Co.   SER 875

Type:	Inverted vertical triple expansion
Photo taken:	1957
Maker and Date:	Buckley & Taylor, Oldham, 1906
Cylinder/dimensions:	24in – 39in – 63in x 4ft 6in – Corliss valves
Hp: 1,800	*Rpm:* 75 *Psi:* 180
Service:	Cotton spinning. 36 rope drive. 26ft flywheel.

This was believed to be one of the largest engines of the design made by Buckley & Taylor, and was originally fitted with piston tail rods to each cylinder, but latterly that on the high pressure cylinder had been removed. It is possible that the cylinder had also been renewed then. The plant was regularly fully loaded, having four boilers and sometimes 2,000 hp load. The cylinders were separate (i.e. not coupled in a single block) with all of the valves in line with the crankshaft. The conditions seen in the print are typical of the results secured by good engineers and management, at the end of over fifty years of work except for some Wartime shut down. All was scrapped when the mill was closed about 1958.

113. Farnworth, nr. Bolton, Dove Spinning Co., Egyyptian Mill
SER 263

Type:	Cross compounded double beam
Photo taken:	
Maker and Date:	Unknown c1850
Cylinder/dimensions:	20ft x 6in – Corliss valves 32ft x 6in – Slide valves
Hp: 290	*Rpm:* 32 *Psi:* 110
Service:	Cotton Mill drive. Gear drive off fly wheel rim to 6ft 0in pinion. Flywheeel 2ft 0in diameter.

This had several alterations as, built as a twin cylinder, it certainly had been McNaughted, as the stools for the high presure cylinders were still in position. New beams by Musgrave had been fitted (name on beams), but it is probable that Hicks supplied the cylinders at the conversion to cross compound. The mill gearing did not appear to have been altered. The mill closed in 1945.

114. Farnworth, Century Ring Mill   SER 1094

Type:	Horizontal cross compound
Photo taken:	1962
Maker and Date:	Hick, Hargreave & Co., Bolton, No. 901, 1900
Cylinder/dimensions:	$26^3/_4$in and 54in x 5ft 0in – Corliss valves
Hp: 1,400	*Rpm:* 70 *Psi:* 180
Service:	Cotton spinning. Ring frames, driven by belts from room mainshafts.

Century Mill was interesting in that it was a four-floored mill, with the engines placed at a high level so that most of the ropes drove downwards from the flywheel. The engine was a typical large Hick, Hargreaves design, with girder frames, and Spencer-Inglis trip gear. The flywheel was large and wide for the power developed, i.e. it had 45 ropes, whereas many 1,400 h.p. engines had 30 or less. Four boilers were provided originally, but with the heavy loads it carried, another boiler by Musgrave was added later. It was another good mill, well loaded. Motor ring frames were installed later, when the engine was scrapped. It certainly paid its way for over 60 years.

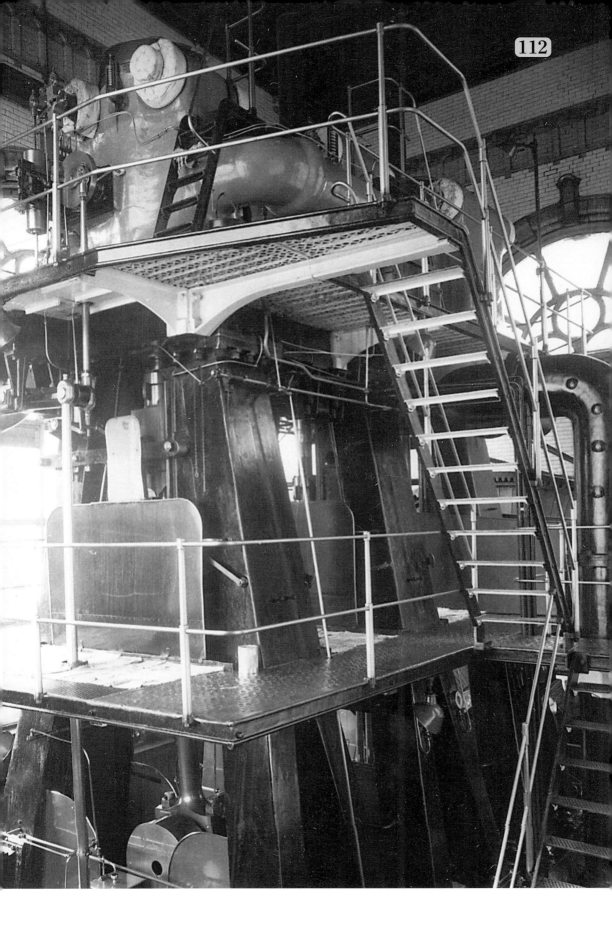

114

115. Finsthwaite, Coward's Bobbin Mill   SER 1246

Type:	Horizontal single cylinder
Photo taken:	1966
Maker and Date:	W. Bradley, Brighouse, 1880
Cylinder/dimensions:	12in x 2ft 0in – Slide valve
Hp: 30?	*Rpm:* 70 *Psi:* 70
Service:	Textile bobbin makers' plant. Auxiliary to water power.

The site was a corn mill, with a large water wheel at first but probably went into bobbin making in the 1850s or earlier. An extension was built on in 1880, and the steam engine was installed to assist the water power. The water wheel was replaced at some time not known by a Gilkes water turbine, possibly horizontal, and this in turn was later replaced by an Armfield water turbine. Both of the turbines were coupled-in by gears and belts to the mill mainshaft, all of the machines being belt driven. The heavy demand for wooden bobbins for the textile trade must have greatly helped these country areas which made a useful product from timber otherwise of little value except for charcoal making. All of the machinery was electrically driven in the 1960s, but with the general decline in the textile the business closed. The mill is now preserved as the Stott Park Bobbin Mill.

116. Facit, Whitworth, Thos: Hoghton, Whitfield Mill   SER 1229

Type:	Horizontal cross compound
Photo taken:	1966
Maker and Date:	Yates & Thom, Blackburn, 1909
Cylinder/dimensions:	19in and 38in x 3ft 0in – Corliss valves
Hp: 500	*Rpm:* 82 *Psi:* 160
Service:	Cotton weaving. 13 rope drive to shed shaft.

This was an old textile plant, and reorganised and equipped by new owners in 1907. The plant had been altered; new machinery with motor drives had required the installation of an alternator which latterly took about one third of the load. There was probably a beam engine once, driving to where the engine condenser was later. The engine was as built, and unusual for a Yates & Thom mill engine in having trunk frames and bored guides, whilst the condenser on the engine room level, too, was unusual. The engine had been well maintained, and given good service certainly for 60 years when photographed, but progressive conversion to motor drives was probable. There was a boiler feed pump driven by a separate eccentric from the crankshaft, again unusual for these builders.

117. Great Harwood, Birtwistle & Fielding   SER 1012

Type:	Multi stage impulse turbine
Photo taken:	1959
Maker and Date:	Hick, Hargreaves & Co., Bolton, 1927
Hp: 1,250	*Rpm:* 130 *Psi:* 5,600
Service:	Cotton spinning. 25 rope drive to floors through reduction gear. Turbine – 5,600 rpm Rope pulley – 360 rpm

This was said to have been purchased from the great Wembley Empire Exhibition of 1924, although the date 1927 was on the pressure-gauge board. There were 7 impulse expansion stages in the turbine, and it drove through double helical toothed gearwheels with a reduction of $18\frac{1}{2}$ to 1 to the 5 feet diameter rope pulley for the four mill floors. The gearing was supplied by the Power Plant Co. of Middlesex. The mill was previously driven by two horizontal engines and massive gearing, and the turbine was very economical, but latterly with light load (500 hp) the steam chest pressure was only 60 psi. The pulley centres for the top floor were said to be the longest in a Lancashire mill, nearly 175ft. The business was closed and all scrapped by the 1960s.

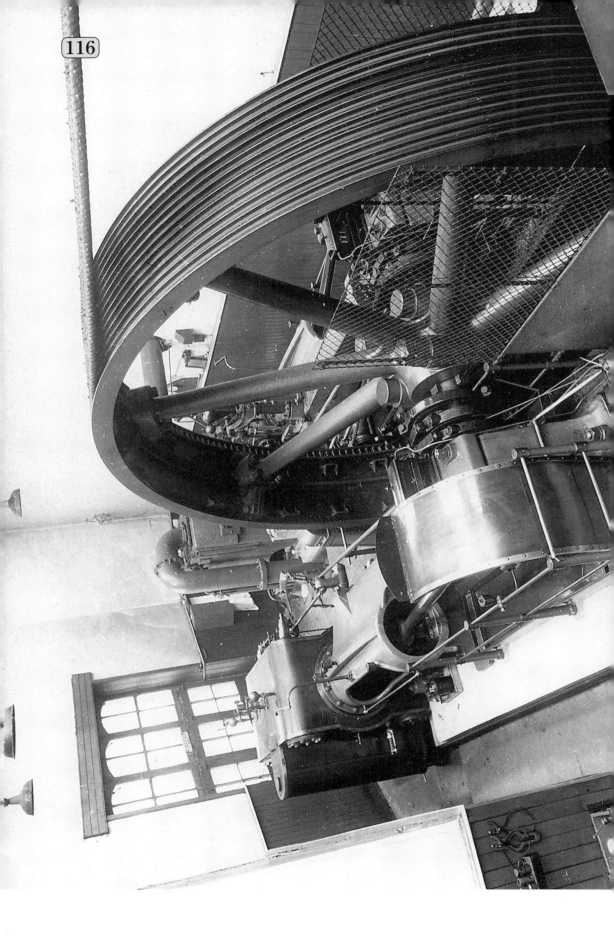

118. Haslingden, Carr, Parker & Co.   SER 1336

Type:	Horizontal single tandem condensing
Photo taken:	1968
Maker and Date:	S. S. Stott and Co., Haslingden, 1908
Cylinder/dimensions:	15in and 27in x 3ft 6in – Corliss and slide valves
Hp: 350	*Rpm:* 85 *Psi:* 120
Service:	Cotton weaving.

A typical Stott & Co engine, this replaced a beam engine in 1908, to drive the attractive little plant which besides weaving some 3,500 yards of cloth per week, prepared much of the yarn, having a complete spinning plant. Rope driving replaced the gear drives of the beam engine at the change of engines, and to gain length for this the engine house was outside the mill. It was quiet and highly efficient, with the Benn patent condenser and air pump at the side of the engine, driven by the ropes and small pulley seen near the wall beyond the flywheel. In this design, the air pump had a very short stroke, and was surrounded by the condenser itself. They were almost noiseless, giving high vacuum with little power to drive it. The closure and scrapping of the plant (c. 1970) was a pity as it was an attractive and very useful business, giving good employment to a variety of craft folks, and with its single oil fired boiler, neat and attractive in every way.

119. Haslingden, The Grane Manufacturing Co.   SER 789

Type:	Horizontal cross compound condensing
Photo taken:	1956
Maker and Date:	S. S. Stott & Co., Haslingden, 1907
Cylinder/dimensions:	18in and 36in x 4ft 0in – Corliss valves
Hp: Approx. 600	*Rpm:* 61 *Psi:* 130
Service:	Cotton weaving.

Another engine which was still running in 1972, and unaltered in over 65 years of work, with very little but minor repairs necessary. The drive was by 16 ropes to the shed mainshaft, which was 390ft. long with 30 pairs of bevel wheels for the loom cross shaft drives. It was a tribute to the good engineers, a family tradition there, and good management which provided well for the engine with stores and time.

120. Haslingden, Hutch Bank Mfg. Co., Grove Mill   SER 157a

Type:	Single McNaught beam
Photo taken:	1935
Maker and Date:	J. Petrie & Co., Rochdale, 1895
Cylinder/dimensions:	21in x 2ft 6in – Corliss and piston valve
	28¾in x 5ft 0in – Slide valve
Hp: 230	*Rpm:* 39 *Psi:* 90
Service:	Cotton weaving 520 looms. Gear drive 12ft to 4ft 6in pinion. 23 loom shafts. Beam 14ft 6in long. Flywheel 15ft 0in diameter. Scrapped 1940?

This was a pure Tattersall design, with the machine-made parallel motion, Corliss inlet and piston exhaust valves, one of several similar made at the time. An interesting feature was that the governor was on the second motion, not the crank shaft. The Tattersall & Baxter trip gear had been replaced by a secondhand Spencer-Inglis set.

121. Haslingden, Warburton and Co., Sykeside Mill   SER 982

Type:	Horizontal single tandem
Photo taken:	1959
Maker and Date:	C. Whittaker and Co., Haslingden, 1900?
Cylinder/dimensions:	19in and 38in x 4ft 0in – Corliss valves
Hp: 600	*Rpm:* 80 *Psi:* 160
Service:	Cotton weaving. 14 rope drive from 16ft flywheel.

This was Whittaker & Co's larger design, which differed little from the smaller ones except that Corliss valves were fitted to both cylinders. The engine was not named, but very well kept. Electrical drives were gradually installed in the early 1960s, and the engine was finally stopped around 1964, and then scrapped. It was typical of the Haslingden-made engines, which were of massive proportions, everywhere. Whittaker & Co usually cast their name on the engine bedplate.

122. Haslingden, Whittaker & Sons, Holme Spring Mill   SER 159

Type:	McNaughted single beam
Photo taken:	1935
Maker and Date:	Unknown, rebuilt 1895
Cylinder/dimensions:	20in x 2ft 6in – Corliss valves
	25in x 5ft 0in – Slide valve
Hp: 220	*Rpm:* 42 *Psi:* 150
Service:	Cotton weaving. Gear drive off flywheel rim, to 6ft 0in pinion. Beam 15ft 0in long. Flywheel 15ft 0in diameter. Scrapped 1950?

Probably rebuilt after a major breakdown. S. S. Stott supplied a new beam, connecting rod, cylinders, and entablature in 1895. This greatly increased the power but it was not enough, as in 1907 a Stott tandem was placed beside it, with a rope drive to the mainshaft, which was then split into two sections, one for each engine.

123. Haslingden, A. Worsley & Sons Ltd., Plantation Mills   SER 913

Type:	Horizontal single tandem
Photo taken:	1958
Maker and Date:	S. S. Stott & Co., Haslingden, 1881
Cylinder/dimensions:	Approx. 16in and 36in x 3ft 6in – Corliss and slide valves
Hp: 300	*Rpm:* 60 *Psi:* 115
Service:	Cotton spinning and weaving. Gear and shaft drive.

This was the oldest remaining Stott & Co engine, and was possibly built as a single cylinder engine in 1881, and compounded later, as there was a rear extension attached to the engine bed carrying the high pressure cylinder, but it may have been built in this way for easier handling on the site. The jaw end of the connecting rod and the four bar cross-head guides were old features in Stott's engines, which were later made as in SER 912, but the governor appeared to be later in date than the rest of the engine. The whole engine story was very confused however, but it was certainly old for a Stott. The mahogany lagging remained on the low pressure cylinder barrel. The load was gradually turned over to motors, but the mill was closed before any value was secured from them. It was interesting that the original Thos. Beeley boiler of 1881 was still insured and ran at 115 psi when 70 years old.

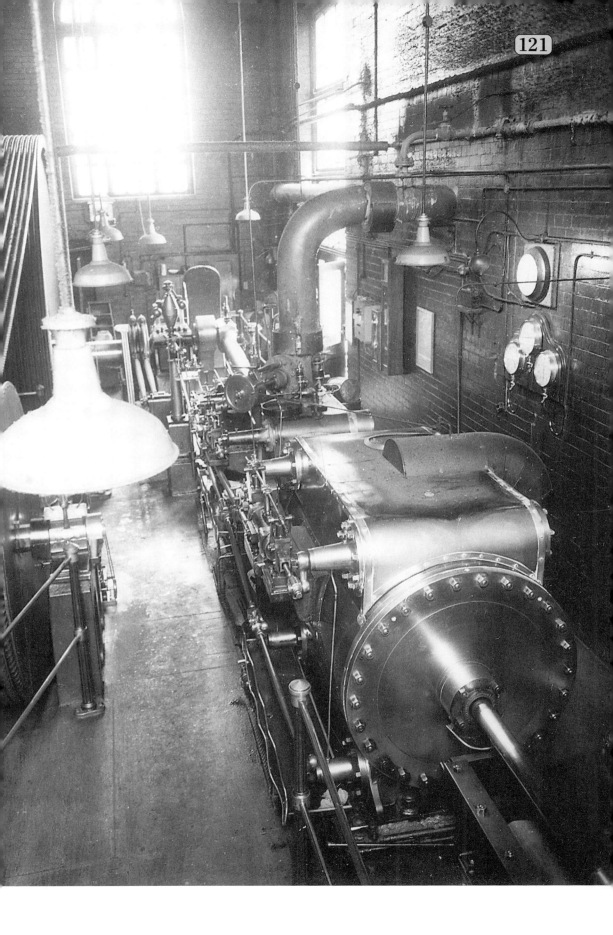

124. Haydock, Richard Evans & Sons Colliery Workshops   SER 545

Type:	Single cylinder condensing beam
Photo taken:	1953
Maker and Date:	Unknown
Cylinder/dimensions:	24in x 5ft 0in – Slide valves
Hp:	*Rpm:* *Psi:*
Service:	Once a haulage engine for Edge Hill railway incline?

This latterly drove the sawmills for the colliery group and was said to have come from Edge Hill incline. It was a plain well-made engine which had needed little major repair. It had been little altered and retained the early type packed back "D" slide valve, but the piston rod glands had possibly been altered, as they were screwed in, whereas the original ones would probably be cottered or eye bolt fixed.

125. Haydock, Wood Colliery   SER 1332a

Type:	Double cylinder horizontal
Photo taken:	1968
Maker and Date:	Robert Daglish & Co., St. Helens, No. 758, 1891
Cylinder/dimensions:	18in x 4ft 0 in – Slide valves
Hp: ?	*Rpm:* 60 *Psi:* 80 (boilers 145 p.s.i.)
Service:	Coal winding. Shaft 480 yards deep. Drum 9ft diameter. No. 3 shaft.

This was an old engine which after many years work was removed to Wood Colliery when the King, Queen and Princess collieries of Richard Evans & Co. were worked out and closed, possibly in the 1930s. It was of an old design, with slide valves on the top of the cylinders, forked or jaw type connecting rod crosshead end. It had very little alteration when moved, except for the addition of the usual safety fittings, and it was certainly a near approach to the original horizontal designs (which followed the beam engines) that remained in every day use a century later.

126. Haydock, Wood Colliery   SER 1332

Type:	Horizontal double cylinder
Photo taken:	1968
Maker and Date:	Stevenson & Co., Preston, 1890s
Cylinder/dimensions:	36in x 6ft 0in – Cornish valves
Hp: ?	*Rpm:* 45 *Psi:* 90
Service:	Coal winding. Shaft 500 yards deep. Rope drum 18ft diameter. No. 4 shaft.

Stevensons were general engineers who did a very wide range of work, but they only built two winding engines, the other one going to the Boston pit not far from No. 4 shaft. The pay-load at No. 4 was 6 tubs containing 4 tons 10 cwt. of coal, making $25^1/_2$ revolutions per wind. Well made, it gave very little trouble. A new steel drum was fitted, but little else was altered when, with the closure of the pit, all the plant was scrapped in 1972. Like Parsonage pit, this was a tribute to the versatility of the Lancashire engineers in that entering a new field, i.e. winding engines, Stevensons like Galloway at Parsonage proved adaptable by building a very good engine when very specific capabilities were needed. Certainly this was a good strong engine with plenty of metal everywhere, and this paid good dividends at Wood pit.

127. Helmshore, L. Whittaker & Sons, Woollen Mills   SER 844

Type:	Middle breast waterwheel
Photo taken:	1956
Maker and Date:	Unknown
Service:	Cloth fulling.

This was an early waterpower site, which was in use until replaced by motor drives in 1955. The waterwheel was interesting in that there were drives taken from each end by gear rings upon the edges, one with internal and the other with external teeth. Mill machinery was driven from the external toothed ring at the other end of the wheel. The whole had been heavily used as the wear on the teeth shows. From the internal teeth the drive was taken below the floor by 6in cast iron shafting to six sets of fulling stocks identical to those in the print. It all remained unaltered making a good product until, when the business was closed in the 1960s, the premises were adapted for an industrial museum.

128. Heywood, Collins Bros., Twin Mill   SER 1148

Type:	Horizontal single tandem	
Photo taken:	1964	
Maker and Date:	Possibly Mills, Heywood, 1880s?	
Cylinder/dimensions:	18in and 30in x 4ft 0in – Slide valves	
Hp: 300	*Rpm:* 48	*Psi:* 130
Service:	Cotton weaving. Gear drive.	

Little positive was known of the history of the plant. It was probably built with a single cylinder engine then converted to tandem compound, with a Corliss valve high pressure cylinder added behind, about 1900, by Rileys of Heywood. The boiler was by Mills, dated 1901, and was their design with seven flue tubes at the back of the flue, instead of the usual style of the flue continuing to the end of the boiler. The engine was parallel to the weaving shed, and drove through heavy bevel wheels to the shed mainshaft, and probably was arranged thus at the start. There did not appear to have been a beam engine. The mill was probably closed in the 1960s, when trade declined.

129. Heywood, J. Kenyon & Son, Crimble Mill   SER 900

Type:	Horizontal tandem extraction engine	
Photo taken:	1958	
Maker and Date:	John Musgrave & Sons (1913) Ltd., Bolton, 1924	
Cylinder/dimensions:	17in and 28in x 2ft 0in – Drop valves	
Hp: 500	*Rpm:* 167	*Psi:* 180
Service:	Textile finishing works. Electric drive.	

This almost certainly the last engine that Musgrave & Sons made for a mill, and indicates how the quality in engine building was maintained, even when the shops were empty of work and men. It was arranged to pass out large quantities of steam at 20 psi, from the receiver between the high and low pressure cylinders, and was fitted with control gear which permitted any variation in steam or electrical load to occur with constant speed. It was regularly used for about 35 years, but in later years heavier loadings, and the need to use steam direct to the processing led to less use and finally all the loads were direct from boilers and Grid by 1963, and the engine was dismantled some years later. One interesting point was that Musgrave name was on the patent stop motion for remote control of the engine in case of accident.

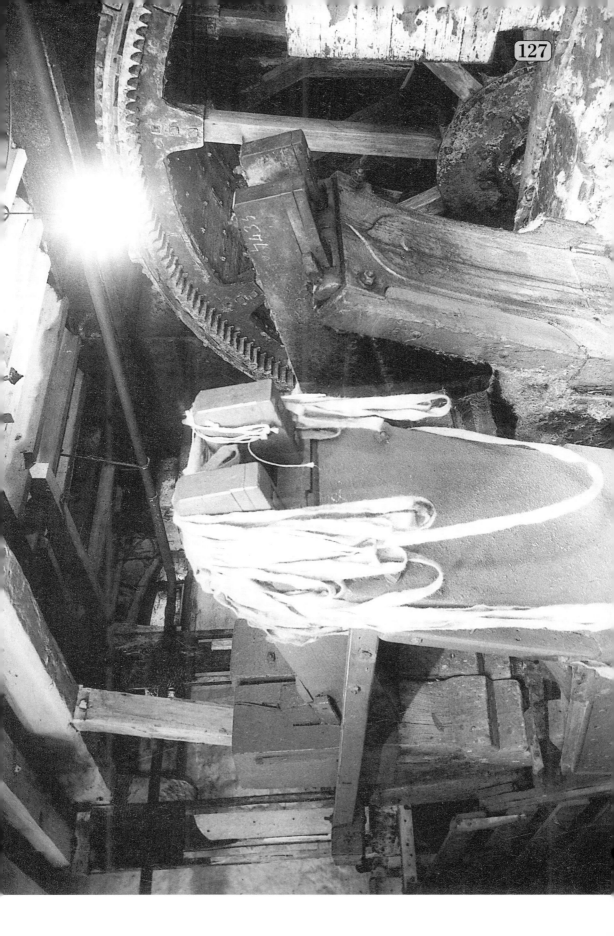

129

130. Hoghton, Southworth, Moore & Co.   SER 827

Type:	Mill buildings
Service:	Cotton weaving

This was a very old water powered site, which still largely used water in the 1950s, when one mill was all electrically driven, but the other still used a water turbine assisted in low water by a single cylinder condensing steam engine. The engine was largely a one man product, by J. H. Bury, who ran a small shop with his son at Oswaldtwistle. It was made in 1910. Very plain, the cylinder was about 10in bore x 1ft 0in with metallic packing and a condenser. The mills were closed in the late 1960s and all sold. It was the last of the old style plants where there were looms upon the upper floors; latterly it was customary to have looms only upon the ground floor.

131. Hollinwood, Gordon Mill   SER 806

Type:	Horizontal twin tandem condensing	
Photo taken:	1956	
Maker and Date:	Buckley and Taylor, 1885	
Cylinder/dimensions:	22in and 50in x 6ft 0in – Corliss and slide valves	
Hp: 1,800	*Rpm:* 45	*Psi:* 160
Service:	Cotton spinning. Gear drive. Mule spinning.	

This was the maker's standard twin tandem slide valve design of which they supplied many for the heavy spinning mill drives in Oldham. Most of these were re-modelled in the early 1900s to give higher power and economy to compete with the new mills being built. Gordon Mill was thus re-modelled by the installation of a new boiler for 160 psi (originally 100 psi) and the Corliss valve high pressure cylinders as seen in the right hand corner. The engine remained structurally as built, only the high pressure cylinders and governor being altered. The drive was by a gear ring on the flywheel rim. The Corliss cylinders were rebored in 1950, and one replaced in 1953, the mill closing in the redundancy scheme of 1960, when all was scrapped. In other occupancy, the buildings were used as storage, but severely damaged by fire in about 1968. As a cotton spinning unit it was very successful.

132. Hollinwood, The Lancashire Cotton Corp., Fox Mill   SER 648

Type:	Single Manhattan compound	
Photo taken:	1954	
Maker and Date:	George Saxon Ltd., Manchester, 1909	
Cylinder/dimensions:	28in and 56in x 4ft 6in – Corliss valves	
Hp: 1,800	*Rpm:* 75	*Psi:* 160
Service:	Cotton spinning. Rope drive.	

The Fox Mill was designed as a double mill, to have two engines, but the other half was never completed. It was unusual in that a double-webbed crank was fitted; most Manhattan engines had a single web or °half crank only. The horizontal low pressure cylinder was the general practice with English Manhattan engines, whereas the low pressure was usually vertical in the U.S.A. Provision was made for the second mill by a 250ft chimney, with space for seven boilers, but only five were installed. The mill was re-equipped with electrically-driven ring spinning frames about 1964 and the engine was then scrapped.

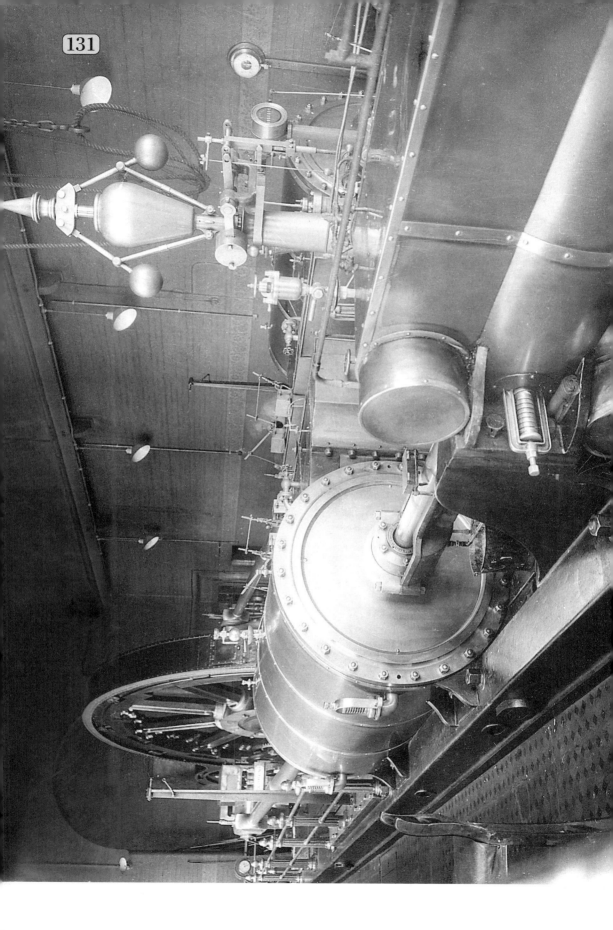

133. Hollinwood, Durban Mill   SER 1063

Type:	Horizontal four cylinder triple expansion
Photo taken:	1961
Maker and Date:	Yates and Thom, Blackburn, 1906
Cylinder/dimensions:	28in – 39in and 2 x 43in x 5ft 0in – stroke, Corliss valves
Hp: 1,750	*Rpm:* 72 *Psi:* 180
Service:	Cotton spinning. 38 rope drive off 26 ft flywheel.

Durban Mill was a very successful mill, which at times loaded the 1,750 hp engine to 2,300 hp. The engine and engine room were highly attractive with fine coloured tiles. The engine was named *Edward* and *Alexandra*, said to be from a Royal visit. Four Tetlow boilers carrying 180 psi originally, still did so when 55 years old. Built as a mule spinning mill it was gradually converted to ring spinning in the 1950-60 period, when an alternator from the Willow Bank mill was installed to provide current. The conversion to ring frames was completed by 1963, and the engine was scrapped, as current was then taken from the Grid.

134. Hollinwood, The Lancashire Cotton Corp., Magnet Mill SER 1093

Type:	Horizontal twin tandem
Photo taken:	1962
Maker and Date:	George Saxon Ltd., Manchester, 1903
Cylinder/dimensions:	$20^{1}/_{2}$ in and $44^{1}/_{4}$ in x 5ft 0in – Corliss valve
Hp: 1,700	*Rpm:* 60 *Psi:* 180
Service:	Ring frames. Cotton Spinning. 35 ropes off 26ft flywheel.

Magnet mill had a typical Saxon engine of the early 1900s but the steam pressure was higher than was usual with compound engines, at 180 psi. It gave the usual Saxon service and was usually heavily loaded by the successful mill. The mill and engines were well-kept and highly attractive in the light engine room. The mill was used for many years after the Lancashire Cotton Corporation owned it, but it was finally closed in the 1960s and all was scrapped. There were five boilers which still carried the original pressure when 60 years old. It was converted later to ring spinning and ran so for many years until the closure.

135. Hollinwood, Nile Mill   SER 102a

Type:	Double triple expansion beam
Photo taken:	1935
Maker and Date:	Buckley & Taylor, Oldham, 1898
Cylinder/dimensions:	2 32in x 3ft 6in – Corliss valves
	2 38in z 4ft 9in – Slide valves
	2 52in x 7ft 0in – Ditto
Hp: 2,400	*Rpm:* 38 *Psi:* 170
Service:	Cotton spinning (medium counts). All main mill drives by bevel gearings and shafts. Spur flywheel for main drive to second motion shaft. 5 boilers 32ft x 8ft 0in built for 160 psi. Mill closed and all scrapped 1960.

Nile was the last, and, with 104,000 ring spindles, the largest, geared cotton spinning mill to be built, whilst the engines were the most powerful beam engines to be designed for a cotton mill. The engines were J. H. Tattersall's design, with a complete triple expansion engine to each beam. The high pressure cylinders were

Continued on page 200...

Continued from page 196...

near to the cranks, McNaught style, with the intermediate and low pressure cylinders at the other end of the beams. The engines were placed between the North and the South mills, as they were called (although the buildings were continuous) and were built to drive three floors. Due to overloading, the top floors were taken off the engine, and the two halves were for over 50 years driven by a 100 hp and a 500 hp motors. The vertical driving shafts were nearly in the centre of the mill.

136. Hollinwood, Nile Mill   SER 102b

Type:
Photo taken:
Maker and Date:
Cylinder/dimensions:
Hp: *Rpm:*   *Psi:*
Service:

The intermediate and the low pressure cylinders were together at one end of the beam, and were outside the main mill wall line. The left hand side was called *Elsie*, the right hand one *Lucy*.

137. Hollinwood, Nile Mill   SER 102c

Type:
Photo taken:
Maker and Date:
Cylinder/dimensions:
Hp: *Rpm:*   *Psi:*
Service:

J. H. Tattersall parallel motion was of modern design and machine-made throughout, with all of the brasses fitted into solid forged box ends; there were none of the usual loose straps, held in place by gibs and cotters. The photograph shows the intermediate and low pressure piston rods of *Elsie* and *Lucy*, whilst *Lucy's* slide valve chest can also be seen.

138. Hollinwood, Nile Mill   SER 102d

Type:
Photo taken:
Maker and Date:
Cylinder/dimensions:
Hp: *Rpm:*   *Psi:*
Service:

The flywheel was a typical Tattersall design with round arms. The construction was closely specified regarding material and fitting up. The toothed rim was 23ft 4in in diameter, with 120 teeth 21in wide x $5^1/_2$in pitch cut in the rim sectors, and this drove to a pinion (on the second motion shaft) 8ft 6in in diameter, which consisted of a steel toothed rim with 54 teeth held to the cast iron boss by steel hoops shrunk on. The vertical shafts were of the marine type, having the couplings forged with the shafts.

139. Hollinwood, The Lancashire Cotton Corp., Royd Mill   SER 649

Type:	Inverted vertical triple expansion
Photo taken:	1954
Maker and Date:	J. & E. Wood, Bolton, 1907
Cylinder/dimensions:	18½in – 28½in – 43in x 3ft 6in – Corliss valves
Hp: 950	*Rpm:* 94 *Psi:* 160
Service:	Cotton spinning. 20 rope drive.

Royd Mill was interesting in that the intermediate pressure cylinder had no front column, the weight there being carried from the end ones by a massive girder casting from the outer ones. The raised circular mouldings on the staircase sides were a J & E Wood feature. J. & E. Wood sometimes put the Corliss valves in the corners of the cylinders in vertical engines, whereas all of the horizontal ones had the Corliss valves below. Royd Mill was converted to electrical drive in 1961, and the engine scrapped.

140. Hollinwood, The Lancashire Cotton Corp., Royd Mill   SER 649a

Type:	Data as SER 649

This is the rear view of the engine, showing that the three back columns are identical, i.e. that there is not an open frame for the centre cylinder as there is in the front of the engine. It also shows that the J & E Wood-type Corliss gear is used as in their horizontal engines. This also shows the circular mouldings which J & E Wood often placed on the stairways, and platform edges, but the handrail standards are plain turned steel, not fluted castings, as they often were in the horizontal engines.

141. Horwich, Montcliff Colliery   SER 1231

Type:	Horizontal single cylinder
Photo taken:	1966
Maker and Date:	Unknown, 1872?
Cylinder/dimensions:	15in x 3ft 0in – Slide valve
Hp: ?	*Rpm:* 40 *Psi:* 100
Service:	Small mine licensed by Coal Board. Man winding and escape shaft. 120 yards deep. The Old Shaft.

This was the original engine driving the winding drum by gearing, and was unaltered. The Old shaft was also the pumping shaft, with the Davey single cylinder horizontal engine (Seen in the far corner of the engine room) working the pump rods which went down the side of the shaft. The cost of installing the pump nearly ruined the little mine in the 1880s, but it kept on by closest economy. Coal drawing was later from the newer shaft, sunk in 1892, with a double cylinder engine 11in x 1ft 6in with a 4ft drum. There was a single Cornish boiler by Andertons, Accrington, which was fired by the winding engine driver. One tub of coal was wound at a time. There was also a boiler, later condemned and taken out, for the Old Shaft and one by Hill, Heywood (probably secondhand) was put in. The little plant ran into the 1960s, but later the mine was closed.

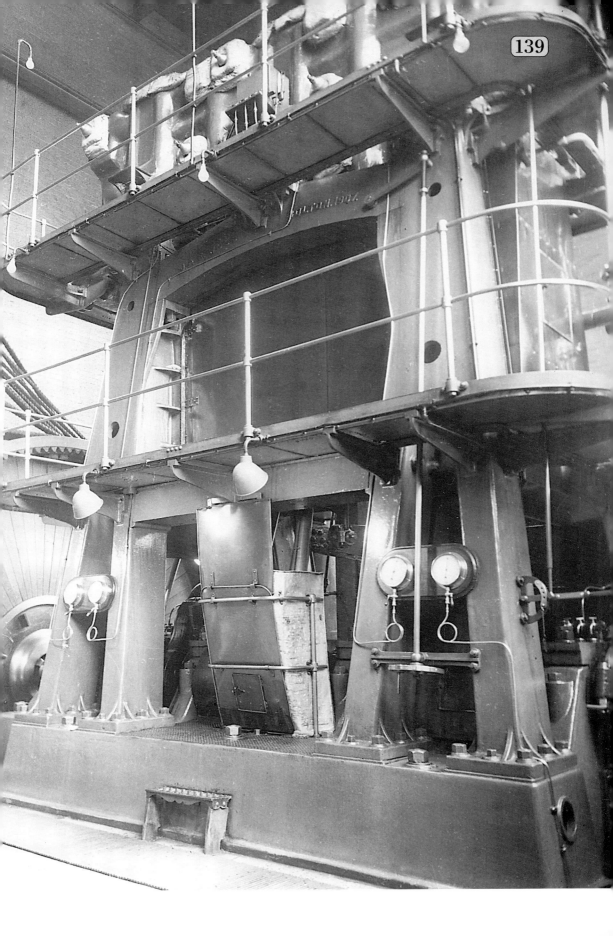

142. Ince, nr. Wigan, The Ince Forge Co.   SER 708

Type:	Vertical boilered locomotive
Photo taken:	1955
Maker and Date:	Wilkinson & Co., Wigan? Date unknown
Cylinder/dimensions:	8in x 10in – Slide valves
Hp:	*Rpm:* *Psi:*
Service:	Works haulage.

This was a typical steam tramway engine, much used for indifferent tracks, and possibly steam tramways, in the latter part of the 19th century. The print shows the unusual engine design with the engine frame across the main frames of the locomotive, and the gear drive to the axle. The counter-balanced cranks, and angle split valve chest covers were practical features. *Owd Ann* as she was called, was in use until the 1950s and believed scrapped soon after. The boiler contained vertical fire tubes, not Field water tubes.

143. Lees, Oldham, The Lees Brook Spinning Co.   SER 854

Type:	Horizontal twin tandem compound condensing
Photo taken:	1957
Maker and Date:	Buckley & Taylor, Oldham, 1886
Cylinder/dimensions:	21in and $48^1/_2$ in x 6ft 0in – Corliss and slide valves
Hp: 1,200	*Rpm:* $35^1/_2$ *Psi:* 160
Service:	Cotton spinning. Geared drive, to vertical shaft.

This was a standard Buckley & Taylors engine of the 1880s, originally fitted with all slide valves and using steam at 100 psi. New high pressure cylinders with Corliss valves were installed in 1905, together with 3 boilers by Edward Heaton of Holt Town, Manchester. The drive was from teeth on the flywheel rim to a pinion on the second motion shaft, 160 teeth on the flywheel rim to 56 on the second motion pinion, and bevel wheels to the vertical shaft and the mill floors. The engine room was within the mill block, and the vertical shaft was almost in the centre of the mill. It was converted to motor drives in 1956.

144. Lees, Oldham, The Lees Brook Spinning Co.   SER 854b

Type:	Vertical shaft and bearing frame
Photo taken:	1957
Maker and Date:	
Cylinder/dimensions:	
Hp:	*Rpm:* *Psi:*
Service:	Part of old drive gearing and room on the right.

The load on this and the floor above had been taken by motors, such as that seen on the framing at the left. The vertical shaft had passed through to the upper floor as well originally, and was 7in diameter at the point seen. Shaft and gearing were encased for safety, and the massive cast iron frame some $2^1/_2$in thick on the wall had carried the bearing above and below the floor drive bevel wheels which were inside the sheet steel casing. The vertical shaft ran at 118 rpm, and the floor or room shaft ran at 204 rpm by a steel bevel wheel with 63 driving to a pinion with 37 teeth on the room shaft. The enlarged part at the floor level encased a muff coupling which had joined the lengths together. All was scrapped when the motors were completed, but it was typical of the heavy gearing needed by the high power of the Oldham coarse count trade.

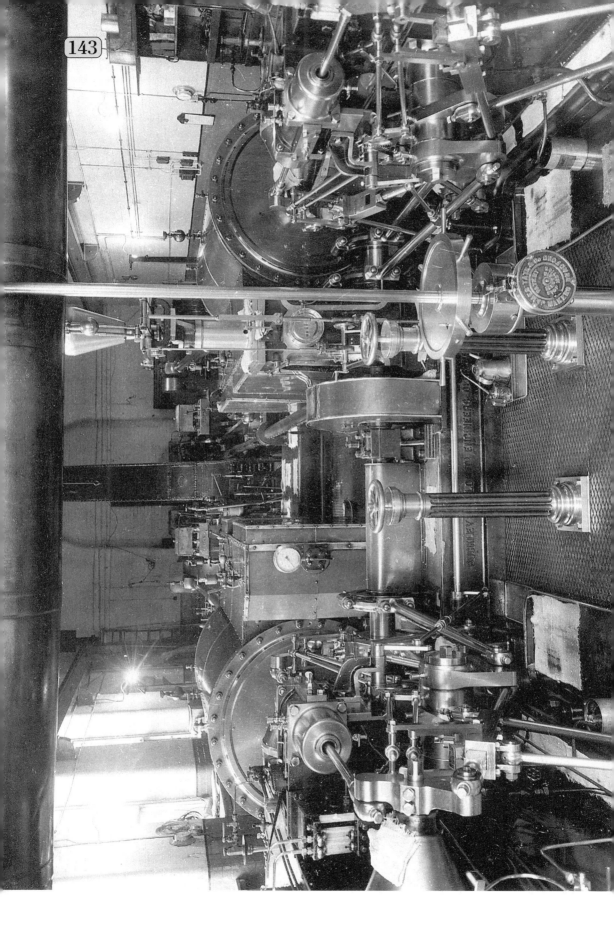

145. Leigh, Bedford Mill   SER 1050

Type:	Horizontal cross compound condensing
Photo taken:	1961
Maker and Date:	J. & E. Wood, Bolton, 1910
Cylinder/dimensions:	27in and 48in x 5ft 0in – Corliss valves
Hp: 1,400	*Rpm:* 75 *Psi:* 160
Service:	Cotton spinning. 32 rope drive to 5 floors.

Again the standard J. & E. Wood design, this was in a plain engine room with neat and modest wall tiling. The drive was by 32 ropes to the five floors, and a Lumb governor had been fitted, probably in the 1920s. The high engine centre line sometimes met in J. & E. Wood engines was evident in this, but otherwise it was the usual good servant Woods built. Two condensers were fitted to this engine, one on each side, and one late repair was the replacement of the white-metal slipper under the high pressure piston in 1950. Electric drives were installed in the 1960s.

146. Leigh, Bickershaw Colliery   SER 1330

Type:	Double cylinder horizontal
Photo taken:	1968
Maker and Date:	John Wood & Co., Wigan, 1880s
Cylinder/dimensions:	36in x 6ft 0in – Slide then piston valves
Hp: ?	*Rpm:* 40 *Psi:* 100
Service:	Coal winding. Shafts 800 yards deep.

A famous colliery, Bickershaw has four shafts, two on electric winders, and No. 1 and No 3 steam in 1973. No. 4 was electrically wound since 1937, and No. 2 had a Robey electric winder of 1956. No. 1 was built with slide valves for 75 psi, and new cylinders by Wood were fitted to allow use of higher steam pressure. It probably dates from 1881, the date of the Walker's winder at No. 3 shaft. Never fitted with tail rods, No. 1 was once run with a skip on one side and a four deck cage on the other rope. The four decks per landing must have slowed operations, but it was wound up to 570 tons per double shift. It was probable that Bickershaw would continue working since it had a coal washer. It was decided to drive a drift to Parsonage pit (SER 1331) many hundreds of yards long to bring the Parsonage pit coal underground to Bickershaw since it could be washed there, to save the great cost of carrying the Parsonage coal by road. It was said that there was no demand for unwashed coal. This probably meant the end of steam at Parsonage pit. When all was on steam there were 24 Lancashire boilers at Bickershaw, with 6 at 160 psi for the No. 4 electrical winder, and 16 at 110 psi for the rest. No. 3 has 3 decks on the cage.

147. Leigh, Brooklands Mill   SER 1052

Type:	Horizontal cross compound condensing
Maker and Date:	J. & E Wood – Bolton – 1893
Cylinder/dimensions:	30$\frac{1}{2}$in and 50in x 6ft 0in –Corliss valves
Hp: 1,200	*Rpm:* 52 *Psi:* 140
Service:	Cotton spinning – mule frames – later driven by motors from engine driven alternator.

A very well kept and efficent unit named *Eudora (high pressure)* and *Cecille (low presure)*, this was of the older slower speed, long stroke, type, and so was a large engine for the power developed. The tiling was attractive, and this was in buff with a deep brown flywheel, which was connected to the cross bar seen above the hand rail. This was to give warning if a driving rope started to fray: the ragged ends would strike the bar and besides ringing the bell, it had also a cross connection which if a serious fray, would stop the engine through the Lumb governor stop motion.

148. Leigh, The Butts Mill Co.   SER 635

Type:	Horizontal cross compound condensing
Maker and Date:	Carels Frères, Ghent – 1906?
Cylinder/dimensions:	32 in and 63 in x 5ft 0in – Drop valves
Hp: 2,500	*Rpm:* 70 *Psi:* 180
Service:	Cotton spinning – Drive by 54 ropes.

There were seven Carels' engines installed in Lancashire spinning mills early in the 20th century. This was probably the work of one architect as in each case the engine rooms were very fine even by the best standards, with ample room everywhere. The engines worked very well. Butts' plant was all scrapped when the mill was closed about 1958, and the premises were occupied by a mail order concern.

149. Leigh, Leigh Spinners Ltd., No 2 Mill   SER 1162

Type:	Horizontal cross compound
Photo taken:	
Maker and Date:	Yates & Thom, Blackburn. 1925
Cylinder/dimensions:	30in and 61in x 5ft 0in – Corliss valves
Hp: 1,800	*Rpm:* 67 *Psi:* 180
Service:	Cotton spinning. 45 rope drive off 24 ft flywheel to 5 floors.

This was certainly the last large engine that Yates & Thom made, and they may have made only two of this size called *Mayor* and *Mayoress*. It was an impressive engine even for Yates & Thom, whose engines never looked as large as they were. The No 1. mill engine was stopped for a number of years following a fractured cylinder, but No 2. ran regularly until the mill closed about 1972, when all the plant was scrapped. There were 7 Lancashire boilers, still carrying 180 psi at the end. Some of the driving ropes rose at a high angle to the floors, and a few were of nylon which, although they cost £105, each ran for years quite untouched.

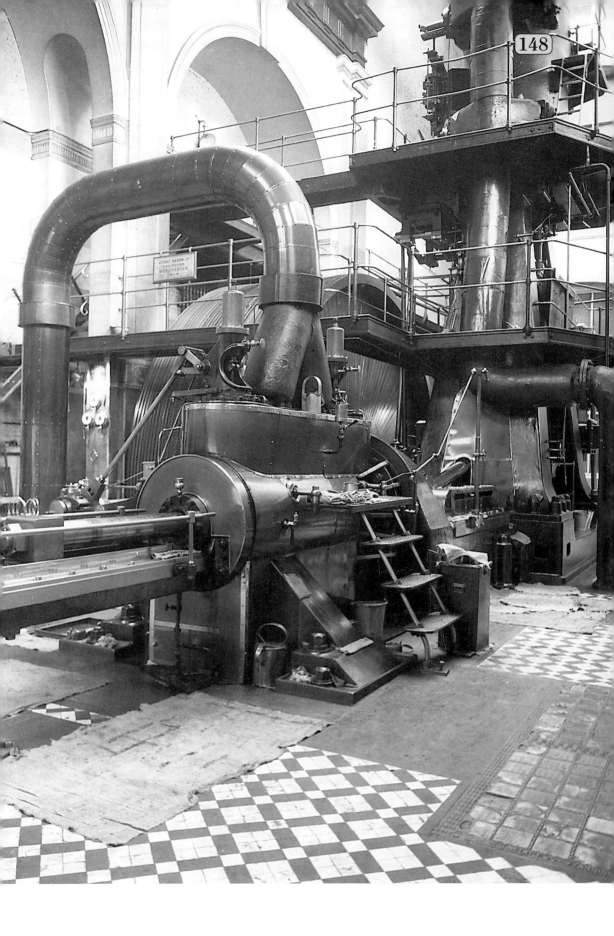

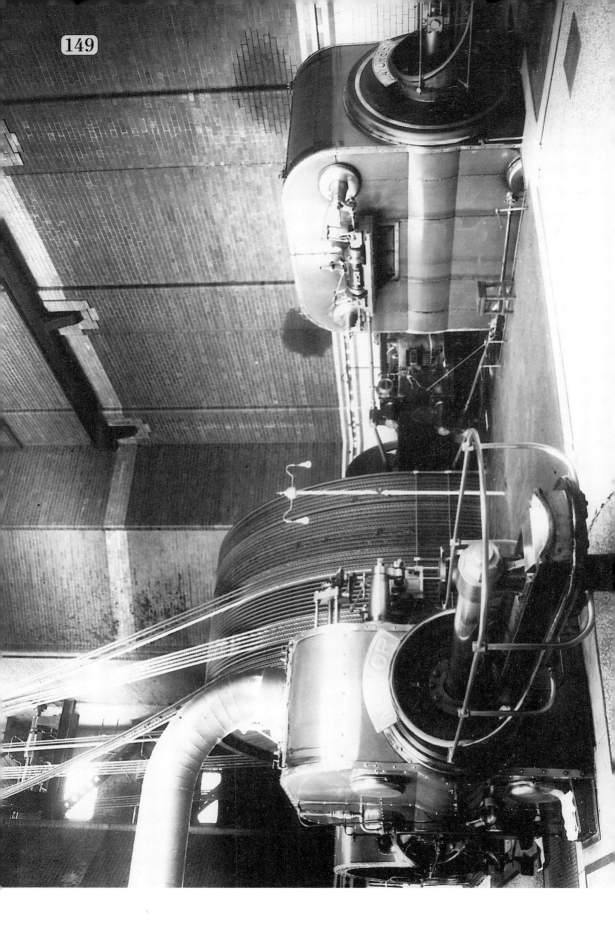

 # SERIES EDITOR, TONY WOOLRICH

Tony was born in Bristol in 1938. He became interested in technical history in his school days, and has been a Member of the Newcomen Society for 40 years, for ten years of which serving as a sub-editor of the *Newcomen Transactions*. He is also a Member of SHOT (the Society for the History of Technology), ICOHTEC (the International Committee for the History of Technology) and the Somerset Archaeological and Natural History Society.

He trained as a craftsman in the engineering industry, and from 1970 has combined his craft and historical skills in modelmaking for museums and heritage projects.

He has also published books and articles on aspects of technical history and biography. A particular interest is industrial espionage of the 18th century. Another interest is 18th century and early 19th century technical books and encyclopaedias, in particular Rees's *Cyclopœdia*, (1802-1819). He has been working on a biography of the engineer John Farey, jr (1791-1851) for the past 20 years.

Since 1989 he has been heavily involved cataloguing for the National Monuments Record, Swindon, the Watkins Collection on the Stationary Steam Engine. He is also a constant consultee to the Monuments Protection Programme of English Heritage.

Since 1994 he has been acting as a contributor to the New *Dictionary of National Biography* working on biographies of engineers and industrialists. He is a contributor to the forthcoming *Biographical Dictionary of Civil Engineers*, published by the Institution of Civil Engineers.

He has recently completed for Wessex Water plc a study of the water supplies of Bridgwater, Wellington (Somerset) and Taunton, and was part of the team setting up the company's education centres at Ashford (near Bridgwater) and Sutton Poyntz (near Weymouth).

ENGINE MAKERS INDEX

Maker	SER No	Plate No
Adamson & Co., D.	1095	110
Ashton, Frost & Co.	1096	109
Ashton, Frost & Co.	1145	98
Ashton, Frost & Co.	716	42
Ashton, Frost & Co.	830	21
Ashton, Frost & Co.	882	17
Ashton, Frost & Co.	902	22
Bracewell & Co., Wm	161	60
Bracewell & Co., Wm	165	78
Bracewell & Co., Wm	168	70
Bradley, W.	1246	115
Buckley & Taylor	854	143
Buckley & Taylor	102a-d	135-8
Buckley & Taylor	177a	79
Buckley & Taylor	177b	80
Buckley & Taylor	177c	81
Buckley & Taylor	498	88
Buckley & Taylor	806	131
Buckley & Taylor	854b	144
Buckley & Taylor	875	112
Burnley Ironworks Co.	1160	69
Burnley Ironworks Co.	1388	51
Burnley Ironworks Co.	699	66
Burnley Ironworks Co.	701	72
Burnley Ironworks Co.	702	75
Burnley Ironworks Co.	914	73
Burnley Ironworks Co.	921	74
Burnley Ironworks Co.	974	59
Carels Frères	635	148
Clayton, Goodfellow	1193	99
Clayton, Goodfellow	611	94
Clayton, Goodfellow	781	23
Clayton, Goodfellow	783	16
Clayton, Goodfellow	828	24
Coates & Co., V.	796	41
Crook T.	1403	27
Crook T.	1403a	28
Daglish & Co.	1332a	125
Daglish & Co., R.	1338	1
Davy Bros	988	13
Duncan, Stewart & Co.	1416a	50
Ferranti Ltd	610	93
Goodfellow, B.	985b	19

Maker	SER No	Plate No
Hathorn, Davy & Co.	158a	56
Hathorn, Davy & Co.	170b	63
Hick, Hargreaves & Co.	834	43
Hick, Hargreaves & Co.	856a	25
Hick, Hargreaves & Co.	1012	117
Hick, Hargreaves & Co.	1021a	30
Hick, Hargreaves & Co.	1094	114
Hick, Hargreaves & Co.	1120b	48
Hick, Hargreaves & Co.	751(2)	31
Hick, Hargreaves & Co.	855	26
Mather & Platt	1416b	49
Mills (?)	1148	128
Musgrave & Sons, J.	1007	7
Musgrave & Sons, J.	900	129
Musgrave & Sons, J.	1028	46
Musgrave & Sons, J.	1183	34
Musgrave & Sons, J.	178	29
Musgrave & Sons, J.	632(1)	84
Musgrave & Sons, J.	632(2)	85
Musgrave & Sons, J.	725a	38
Musgrave & Sons, J.	725b	39
Musgrave & Sons, J.	751(1)	32
Musgrave & Sons, J.	756(3)	4
Musgrave & Sons, J.	780	92
Musgrave & Sons, J.	833	37
Musgrave & Sons, J.	869	76
Petrie & Co., J.	154	10
Petrie & Co., J.	157a	120
Pollit & Wigzell	1101	71
Pollit & Wigzell	1125	68
Pollit & Wigzell	1161	55
Pollit & Wigzell	1165	54
Pollit & Wigzell	705	61
Roberts & Sons, Wm (?)	167b	53
Roberts & Sons., Wm	1100	101
Roberts & Sons., Wm	1126	102
Roberts & Sons., Wm	506b	100
Roberts & Sons., Wm	803	67
Roberts & Sons., Wm	918	77
Roberts & Sons., Wm	979	14
Rushton's Foundry (?)	1404	107
Saxon Ltd, G.	1064	2
Saxon Ltd, G.	1093	134
Saxon Ltd, G.	633a	45
Saxon Ltd, G.	633b	44
Saxon Ltd, G.	648	132
Scott & Hodgson	755	91
Scott & Hodgson	807	3
Sharples, Wm	1147	12
Sharples, Wm	884	104
Shorrock & Co., J. & R.	829	106

Continued over page...

Engine Makers Index continued...

Maker	SER No	Plate No
Stevenson & Co., R.	1332	126
Stott & Co., S. S.	1336	118
Stott & Co., S. S.	789	119
Stott & Co., S. S.	913	123
Stott & Co., S. S.	1123	82
Unknown	155	8
Unknown	1102	9
Unknown	1120a	47
Unknown	1231	141
Unknown	158b	57
Unknown	159	122
Unknown	167a	52
Unknown	170a	62
Unknown	170c	64
Unknown	171	65
Unknown	263	113
Unknown	503	111
Unknown	545	124
Unknown	984	95
Urmson & Thompson	603	89
	793	90
Urmson & Thompson	730	87
Westinghouse Co.	725c	36
Whittaker & Co., C.	883	15
Whittaker & Co., C.	982	121
Wilkinson & Co	708	142
Wood & Co., J.	1330	146
Wood Bros	824	97
Wood Bros	153	11
Wood, J & E	795	40
Wood, J & E	1008	105
Wood, J & E	1158	35
Wood, J & E	715	6
Wood, J & E	1405	108
Wood, J & E	802	96
Wood, J & E	1009	83
Wood, J & E	1050	145
Wood, J & E	1052	147
Wood, J & E	649	139
Wood, J & E	649a	140
Yates & Thom	1063	133
Yates & Thom	1162	149
Yates & Thom	1229	116
Yates & Thom	1337b	58
Yates & Thom	857	33
Yates, W & J	904	86
Yates, W & J (?)	507	103
Yates, W & J	1022	20
Yates, W & J	985a	18

Non Stationary Engine Makers Index

	SER No	Plate No
Locomotive		
Hawthorn & Co	757	5
Waterwheel		
Unknown	844	127
Mill Building		
Southworth, Moore & Co.	827	130

STATIONARY STEAM ENGINES OF GREAT BRITAIN

THE NATIONAL PHOTOGRAPHIC COLLECTION

VOLUME 3.2: LANCASHIRE

George Watkins